TRIBE : *What Covenants Are Governing You—Not Because You Chose Them, But Because You Were Born Into Them?*
by Dr. Marlene Miles

Freshwater Press 2026

Freshwaterpress9@gmail.com

ISBN: 978-1-971933-14-6

Paperback Version

Table of Contents

PREFACE 6

INTRODUCTION..............................7

TRIBE... 14

A CLIQUE IS NOT A TRIBE 17

WHAT IS A SOUL TRIBE?................ 23

WHAT THIS BOOK IS NOT ABOUT 26

TRAUMA BONDS DO NOT MAKE A TRIBE........ 28

BLOOD IS NOT JUST BIOLOGY 29

WHY GOD THINKS IN LINES 33

BLOOD CREATES OBLIGATIONS *AND* PERMISSIONS 37

WHAT WAS SIGNED BEFORE YOU WERE BORN? 42

INHERITED COVENANTS............................... 46

PRAYER FOR MY TRIBE 50

PERMISSIONS YOU DIDN'T APPLY FOR 53

WHEN EVIL COVENANTS GO UNNAMED 57

OTHER TRIBES 61

AM I MY BROTHER'S KEEPER?........................ 65

DO NOT FORSAKE THE GATHERING 68

FAMILY, BLOODLINE, TRIBE............................ 72

TRIBAL JURISDICTION........................ 76

THE SCATTERED TRIBE 81

BLOODLINES MATTER....................... 85

FROM JACOB TO ISRAEL.................... 88

STANDING IN THE GAP FOR A LINE................ 91

CAN YOU FIND YOURSELF IN JACOB? 95

POSITIVE TRAITS OF THE TRIBES OF ISRAEL... 97

THE GENEALOGY OF JESUS......................... 102

DECLARATIVE PRAYER: I AM IN CHRIST........ 104

DECLARATIVE LINE PRAYER — I AM IN CHRIST
(WITH INHERITANCE)................................ 108

Dear Reader 111

Appendix: Common Tribal Distortions When
Strength Is Ungoverned 113

DECLARATIVE LINE PRAYER — I AM IN CHRIST
.... 117

Prayerbooks by this author 120

Prayer Manuals 120

Prayer Manuals 122

Other books by this author 123

TRIBE:

Identity is not accidental.
Belonging is not neutral.
Inheritance is not imaginary.

TRIBE

**WHAT COVENANTS ARE GOVERNING YOU -
-      NOT BECAUSE YOU CHOSE THEM,
BUT BECAUSE YOU WERE BORN INTO
THEM?**

Freshwater

PREFACE

People throw the word, *tribe* around a lot, so this book is to bring clarification to what a tribe really is. First of all, how many people don't even know what country their people hail from? Then how can we know the tribe if we don't even know the country? Do we just pick a tribe? One that sounds cool?

Do we choose a tribe on the land where we now reside, just because?

This book is intended to be an interesting study and appropriate spiritual reset for myself and whoever else finds and reads this book.

One day I was in a congregational prayer, and the Spirit of the Lord told me, "Pray for your tribe." I never considered that I had a tribe, knew of a tribe, and no one in my family ever talked about such. I heard in my spirit, *"tribe.* Pray for your tribe." I did and I got a quickening in my spirit and instant deliverance. Less than a minute later the online pastor said, "Pray for your tribe." Well, that confirmed it.

That was the impetus of this book.

INTRODUCTION

The word **"tribe"** is everywhere right now:

- *Find your tribe*

- *Protect your tribe*

- *My tribe rides with me*

- *Chosen family is my tribe*

We don't want to be among the people using the word "tribe" but have no idea what it actually means in every sense of the word—, historically, culturally, spiritually, or Biblically. When a word loses its definition, it becomes a substitute identity.

This book is not about anthropology, it goes deeper, into **identity amnesia.**

Many people don't know what country their ancestors came from. Where I am from the closest people who speak or think like that would be a Native American tribe; they are the ones with tribes on our side of the world. Many do not know what language their people spoke. One year I decided to learn several languages, and I was amazed at which were super easy for me, and ones that I thought would be easy, were not. I wondered if that had something to do with where my people are from.

Many do not know what customs, laws, or faith patterns shaped them. Yet they speak fluently about their *tribe.*

So, the modern use of the word, *tribe* often becomes a placeholder for belonging. It becomes a social defense mechanism. It can be a spiritual stand-in for lineage, covenant, and inheritance.

Ancestry has two sides, claimed ancestry which we learn about from family stories, oral tradition, and DNA inference. Then there is recognized ancestry when we have documented lineage and we are accepted by a living tribe.

Native American tribes are sovereign political nations, not abstract identities. They define their own membership—usually through documented descent, enrollment rolls, blood quantum, historical records. So, the issue is often jurisdiction, not truthfulness. Someone may *have* Native ancestry and still not belong to a tribe. This book really isn't about local *tribes,* but I use it as an example. Without or without DNA tests, many African American families and I've met some Caucasians who also believe they have Native American ancestry, and perhaps, their tribe is found among Natives. But not all Native Tribes agree with those claims. There are many reasons why not, such as enslavement-era erasure: enslaved people were cut off from records. There could be oral history filled gaps. Intermarriage did occur in some regions since Native American or any other identity became safer than African ancestry in certain historical periods in the United States.

Census and record manipulation blurred categories intentionally. Family survival narratives passed down without documentation. This means history, as life can be, was violent and messy.

Not just Native tribes, but tribes all over the world may not affirm a claim of belonging for many reasons. Native tribes generally resist broad claims because They have been repeatedly erased, exploited, and impersonated. Federal recognition and resources depend on strict enrollment. Loose identity claims threaten sovereignty. Many tribes have their own trauma with blood quantum laws. So, when tribes do not "claim" African Americans (or others) who claim Native ancestry, it is not personal—it is protective governance.

Identity is not the same as inheritance. A person can inherit genetic markers, family stories, and cultural proximity. While at the same time they may not inherit tribal jurisdiction, political belonging, or covenantal responsibility. Blood may be present, but **tribe** requires continuity and recognition. When it

9

comes to African Americans and Native Americans we see deep historical losses in both groups. African Americans lost records, languages, nations. Native Americans lost land, population, recognition. Claims of overlap touch unresolved grief, not just facts.

That's why the conversation often feels explosive—it's not about ancestry alone; it's about who gets to say who *belongs*. Ancestry can be complex, but tribe is defined by living continuity and recognition. One does not automatically create the other.

All this is to say a person can, and should, **pray for their tribe** even if they never know who that tribe is by name. As a matter of fact, you have jurisdiction to pray for anyone in your bloodline, unless they tell you not to pray for them. But pray for your tribe, especially if their line has been displaced, fragmented, renamed, or erased.

Jurisdiction is like a cop's authority. A city cop doesn't have authority past the county line—even if they can see what's happening there.

Spiritually, you can *notice* something outside your jurisdiction, you can even *care* about it, but you can't act there with authority. Spiritually that could mean that you'd have no effect praying for something that is above your pay grade. Or, it could mean that adverse things could happen if you overstep, spiritually.

Jurisdiction means authority with limits—like a cop who must stop at the county line. So, when I prayed for my tribe, I prayed generically, not calling any tribe by name.

Prayer does not require full knowledge to be effective when you are praying with understanding. Of course, if you are praying in the Spirit, the Holy Spirit will help, so just pray. In Scripture, God responds to jurisdictional humility. A person can truthfully pray:

- *"I don't know the names."*

- *"I don't know the covenants."*

- *"I don't know what agreements were made."*

So just pray.

Inherited covenants can affect a person without their consent or awareness. Consequences can travel through generations. Patterns repeat without explanation. Burdens appear without personal cause. That doesn't mean a person is guilty. It means they are standing inside a story they did not start. History has weight, and it carries – unless there's God. Only God has authority over whatever is following you.

Praying without knowing the tribe is actually wise because without naming a tribe, you avoid three dangers: misidentification, romanticizing a lineage, and overstepping authority. Praying in the spirit may be the safest way. Just pray in real submission, with pure surrender and in alignment in your right authority. Yes, there is such a thing as spiritual mapping, but God does not burden you to reconstruct lost ancestry, name forgotten people, solve historical ruptures or solder ancient tribal histories back together.

The burden is on God to govern what is hidden. This is a valid prayer for your tribe, known or unknown:

Father, where covenants were made without my
consent, where obligations still speak,
where patterns persist without explanation—
I place all of it under the authority of Christ.

In the Name of Jesus, Amen.

This type of praying does not lead to obsession—it leads to rest. Done correctly, this kind of prayer does not send people hunting ghosts, instead, it does the opposite. It will settle feelings of: *What's wrong with me?"* And then you'll start saying, *"Something predated me—and God outranks it.*

That day I heard in the Spirit, "Pray for your tribe." I got deliverance. You can pray for yours, also. Not knowing your tribe does not disqualify you from healing. Not knowing your history does not prevent redemption. Christ does not require perfect information—only rightful authority.

A person may never know their tribe, but God still knows the covenants that touched their line—and Christ is sufficient to govern them.

Even if you've gone to the Lord or come to this book thinking:

- *Why does what I'm going through keep repeating?*

- *Why does effort never fully resolve these repetitive issues in my life?*

- *Why does freedom feel partial?*

- *Why do I sense resistance but I don't really know what it is?*

Based on my own experiences, I can say, *You're not imagining it. And you're not required to solve it alone—or even understand it fully.* I encourage you, as the Spirit spoke to me and then it was confirmed by the man of God, "Pray for your tribe."

TRIBE

Most people use the word *tribe* to describe who they feel connected to. This book uses the word to describe who you are responsible for.

In Scripture, tribes were not formed by preference. They were formed by blood, covenant, and obligation. You did not choose the tribe you were born into; you inherited it. Which means you also inherited permissions you did not apply for, responsibilities you did not volunteer for, or covenants you may not yet recognize.

Still, some of those covenants are holy. Some are incomplete. Some were made in fear, famine, or desperation. Some could be evil covenants that are still operating.

This book is not about blame; it is about jurisdiction. God does not see people in isolation. He sees lines. Until you understand the line you stand in, you may keep fighting battles that are not personal, they are inherited.

This book, **TRIBE** is for people who are ready to stop asking, *"Why does this keep happening?"* and start asking, *"What am I standing in the middle of?"*

A true tribe historically involved:

1. **Shared lineage** (blood or adoption)

2. **Shared story** (origin, survival, memory)

3. **Shared law or code** (how disputes are handled)

4. **Shared responsibility** (care for widows, elders, children)

5. **Shared spiritual covering** (God, *gods*, rituals, priesthood)

Biblically, tribes were not vibes, they were accountable units. That's why Scripture tracks Genealogies, inheritances, blessings, curses, exiles, restorations. You cannot understand Scripture deeply without understanding tribal structure.

Many people are forming *"tribes"* to avoid healing, not to deepen belonging. Modern tribes are often built on shared wounds instead of shared responsibility. Some are built on shared enemies instead of shared purpose. Some are made based on shared language of victimhood instead of shared growth. A real tribe corrects you, carries you, remembers you, reminds you of who you are, where you come from, and who your people are if you forget.

Tribe is real family and it does not collapse when feelings change.

Tribe is not who claps for you. Tribe is who is responsible for you. True tribe will catch you if you fall or are falling.

Before you find your tribe, you must know your people.

Ask yourself: *What am I actually longing for when I say the word 'tribe'?*

A clique is not a tribe. Trauma bonds do not make a tribe. And, ultimately, this book will ask and help you answer: *Can you find yourself in Jacob?*

A CLIQUE IS NOT A TRIBE

A clique is built on preference, proximity, performance, and mutual affirmation. A clique asks, *Do you fit us? Do you agree with us? Do you reflect us well?*

A tribe, by contrast, is built on responsibility, continuity, correction, and memory. a tribe asks, *who are you accountable to?" Who carries you when you fail? Who stays when situations are inconvenient?*

Cliques dissolve when status shifts, feelings change, or attention moves elsewhere. Tribes endure because leaving costs something.

This distinction alone dismantles most modern uses of the word, *tribe*. The word *tribe* has been softened by overuse. It is now applied to friend groups, online communities, shared interests, and emotional alliances. People speak of "finding their tribe" the way they speak of finding a favorite restaurant—something that suits them, reflects them, and makes them feel comfortable.

But historically—and biblically—a tribe was never defined by comfort. A tribe was defined by responsibility.

A clique forms around preference.

A tribe forms around obligation.

A clique forms around flesh.

A tribe forms because of blood.

A clique asks, *Do we get along? Do we agree? Do you affirm me? Do you fit here?*

A tribe asks, *Who are you accountable to? Who is accountable to you? What happens to them if you walk away? What happens to you if you fail?*

The difference is not emotional; it is structural.

Cliques are voluntary. Tribes are inherited.

You can leave a clique without consequence. Leaving a tribe fractures something—whether immediately visible or not. This is why modern culture prefers the language of tribes but practices the behavior of cliques. The word carries warmth, but the structure carries no weight.

A clique can and often will dissolve when feelings change, conflict arises, growth diverges, or convenience disappears.

A tribe endures because leaving costs something--, not socially, but covenantally. In Scripture, tribes were not built on shared taste or shared trauma. They were built on blood, covenant, history, law, inheritance, and mutual consequence. This is why tribal identity feels heavy to modern ears.

Weight has fallen out of fashion.

Many people today are not avoiding tribes because they lack belonging, they are avoiding tribes because tribes require answerability.

A clique lets you curate yourself. A tribe remembers who you were before you learned how to curate.

This is also why trauma bonds are often mistaken for tribes. Trauma creates intensity. Intensity creates attachment. But attachment does not equal covenant. Trauma bonds connect people through shared wounds. Tribes connect people through shared responsibility.

If healing threatens the bond, it was never a tribe. It was a coping structure. A tribe does not require pain to survive. It requires continuity. This is why Scripture spends so much time on genealogies, houses, and bloodlines. God is not obsessed with ancestry for sentiment's sake. He is tracking jurisdiction.

- Who belongs to whom.
- Who is responsible for whom.

- Who stands in the gap when something breaks.

This is why the first murder in Scripture is followed immediately by the question, *Am I my brother's keeper?* This is a tribal question, and the implied answer—throughout Scripture—is yes. If you remove responsibility, you don't get freedom. You get fragmentation.

If you remove covenant, you don't get belonging. You get proximity without protection. If you replace tribe with clique, you may feel accepted— but you will not be covered.

This book is not asking you to abandon community. It is asking you to tell the truth about what kind of community you are standing in. Because a clique cannot carry inheritance, trauma cannot sustain continuity; only a tribe can do that.

Cliques are about vibes and atmosphere— controlling the narrative. Tribes are about jurisdiction, authority, and governance.

A clique controls atmosphere. A tribe governs territory. Cliques curate perception. Cliques are for clicks. Tribes carry responsibility.

Atmosphere can be faked. Jurisdiction cannot.

A tribe has jurisdiction because it is responsible for outcomes. A clique has influence because it shapes mood, perception, and belonging—but it does not carry responsibility.

Influence can suggest. Governance can decide. Influence can persuade. Governance can authorize, restrain, or release.

A clique has atmosphere, vibes, and controls the narrative. It has social pressure and controls access. It also moves in approval and exclusion. But a clique does not have lawful authority, accountability for outcomes, and has no responsibility for consequences. That's why cliques dissolve under stress. They were never built to carry weight.

Biblically, an elder at the gate is there to govern, not merely to influence. The gate is a place of judgment, contracts, testimony, a place of dispute resolution. The gate is the place where authority was exercised publicly. An elder didn't sit at the gate to *set the tone,* no they sat there to decide matters that affected the community.

The elder at the gate governs, while the court of public opinion, the online community, the crowd at the gate only influences.

What about those elders in Ezekiel for example who meet under the cover of night? In Scripture, governance is meant to happen in the light, with witnesses and accountability. When something happens quietly, at night, without witnesses, and without formal process, under darkness, that usually signals influence trying to masquerade as authority. True governance does not need darkness to function.

An elder at the gate by day = governance. Decisions made in shadow or secrecy = influence, manipulation, or subversion. Even if the person *holds* a title, legitimate authority governs openly.

Influence operates subtly. When influence tries to act like governance, disorder follows, and that's true anywhere, from tribes to families, churches, organizations and even nations.

A clique influences atmosphere, but a tribe governs outcomes. An elder at the gate exists to govern—and governance does not require secrecy.

WHAT IS A SOUL TRIBE?

Soul tribe is sometimes called a *soul family, or tribe of my soul.*

First know that this book is about none of that, but this chapter is FYI and for your edification. This book is not about ancestors or ancestral worship—not at all.

In every generation, people form tribes that are constructed rather than inherited—and some that are inherited through legacy pledges. These are groups curated around ideology, secrecy, loyalty, initiation, or shared identity. They may appear as movements, societies, fraternities, sororities, clubs, or spiritual communities. Some are social in nature; others carry unspoken vows or expectations of allegiance.

This book does not attempt to catalog such groups. It simply affirms this principle: any tribe, group, or identity—whether chosen or inherited—that requires allegiance, secrecy, or submission that rivals Christ must be approached with discernment.

With or without deities, created "tribes" are cliques. If it didn't start with natural blood and flow through blood by inheritance, it's a clique.

Belonging becomes bondage when it demands loyalty beyond conscience or obedience beyond God.

Soul tribe terminology does *not* originate in Scripture. It originates in modern spiritual, therapeutic, and New Age language, with some later crossover into pop-Christian speech.

1. New Age / metaphysical spirituality (primary origin). The phrase grew out of ideas like soul groups soul families, soul contracts, reincarnational clusters, vibrational alignment. In that framework, people are "connected" by essence or frequency, bonds are formed outside blood, covenant, or history. Belonging is felt, not inherited, permanence is emotional, not moral or covenantal. This is where *soul tribe* first had traction.

Therapy & recovery culture (secondary stream). Later, the term was adopted in trauma recovery spaces, group therapy language, identity-affirming communities. Here it means "people who feel safe to me" "those who understand my wounds". "chosen family." This version is psychological, not spiritual—though it often borrows spiritual tone.

Social media & influencer Christianity (tertiary adoption). Eventually, the phrase slipped into

Christian circles, usually meaning, people I feel aligned with, people who "get me", community without hierarchy or obligation. But here's the key problem Scripture never defines belonging by the soul.

Soul tribe" is theologically unstable Biblically because tribe is defined by blood, covenant, and responsibility. Soul is the seat of mind, will, and emotion—*not* lineage. So "soul tribe" quietly replaces inheritance, preference, covenant, chemistry, responsibility, and resonance. That's why it feels warm but often proves non-durable.

Scripture, instead, speaks in terms of house, father's house, tribe, people, seed, inheritance, covenant and body (in Christ). None of these are emotion-based categories. They all involve obligation, accountability, continuity, and cost.

The idea of a 'soul tribe' is modern, and it's emotional; Scripture defines *tribe* as covenantal, inherited, and accountable.

WHAT THIS BOOK IS NOT ABOUT

A necessary clarification is that this book speaks about lineage, bloodlines, inheritance, and covenant. It does not speak about ancestral *spirits*, ancestral powers, or communication with the dead. Those concepts are not assumed, endorsed, or implied anywhere in this work.

When the Holy Bible refers to ancestors, it refers to historical people, not spiritual intermediaries. When it speaks of inheritance, it speaks of covenants, consequences, blessings, and responsibilities that move through time—not *spirits* that move between worlds. The dead do not govern the living. The dead do not instruct the living. The dead do not protect, guide, empower, or authorize the living. The dead do not become angels.

Authority belongs to God alone.

This book does not teach that ancestors possess spiritual power, awareness, or agency after death. It does not promote ancestral veneration, ancestral guidance, or ancestral mediation of any kind. Any attempt to derive power, insight, protection, or direction from the dead falls outside of both the scope and the foundation of this work.

Modern spiritual language often blurs these distinctions, confusing history with mysticism and inheritance with spiritual access. Scripture does not make that confusion.

Patterns can be inherited. Consequences can be inherited. Covenants can affect generations, but spiritual authority does not pass through the dead.

Redemption does not come through ancestry. Clarity does not come through ancestral contact. Freedom does not come through ancestral alignment. **Redemption comes through Christ alone.**

This book addresses bloodlines only in the way Scripture does: as lines of human continuity in which obedience, disobedience, blessing, and consequence unfold across generations—and are ultimately answered by a greater covenant.

Any practice that seeks spiritual power, knowledge, or protection through the dead is not Divine Wisdom. It is deception. And it is not compatible with the theology, purpose, or prayers contained in this book. **TRIBE** is about responsibility, not reverence. About covenant, not communion with spirits. About clarity, not curiosity. The living answer to God. And God alone governs the line.

TRAUMA BONDS DO NOT MAKE A TRIBE

Trauma bonds feel deep. They are formed by shared pain, shared enemies, shared narratives and memories of harm, and mutual reinforcement of wounds. They sound like, *"Only you understand what I went through. We survived the same thing. Or, They'll never get us."*

Trauma bonds connect wounds, not callings. A tribe does not orbit trauma. A tribe outgrows it.

True tribes do not need pain to stay connected. Real tribes do not punish healing as "betrayal." Authentic tribes do not require stagnation to preserve unity. If growth threatens the bond, it was never a tribe. It was a coping mechanism. That clarification alone may either unsettle you, or set you free. Judge this for yourself, and let God be true.

BLOOD IS NOT JUST BIOLOGY

In modern language, *blood* is treated as data, such as a test result, a percentage, a curiosity. In Scripture, blood is **testimony**. Blood speaks. Blood remembers. Blood binds.

This is why covenant is so often sealed in blood—not because God is violent, but because blood represents **life placed under obligation.** When God looks at a person, He does not see an isolated individual floating free of history. He sees a **line**.

Blood carries memory, authority, obligation, permission or exposure, inheritance. This is not mysticism, this is how Scripture reasons.

This is also why genealogies matter. They are not filler. They are legal records. They answer questions like *Who belongs where? Who has authority to speak here? Who is responsible when something breaks? Who inherits when something is restored?*

Blood establishes **jurisdiction**.

You may not feel loyal to your bloodline. You may not agree with its choices. You may not even know much about it. None of that erases its reach.

Ignorance does not dissolve covenants. Disagreement does not nullify inheritance. Just as in a family, the very thing you may hate about a parent or ancestor, you could inherit it. Your emotions about it won't change it. It is, until you pray and ask the Lord to deliver you. It is, until God says **IT IS NOT**. Amen.

This truth is uncomfortable in a culture that prizes self-definition above all else. But Scripture does not treat identity as self-generated. It treats identity as received, stewarded, and sometimes redeemed.

Blood creates obligations.

This is why the question *"Am I my brother's keeper?"* lands so heavily. It assumes blood carries responsibility whether one wants it or not.

Blood also creates permissions.

There are doors that open because of where you come from. There are battles you are authorized to fight because of your line. There are graces that follow you—not because you earned them, but because someone before you did.

This is why blessings and consequences both travel generationally; it is the blood and blood has continuity. Think of a bloodline as a carrier wave. This also explains why some struggles feel deeply personal—and yet oddly impersonal at the same time.

You fight hard. You pray sincerely. You change patterns consciously. And yet something keeps reappearing. Not because you are failing— but because the issue is older than you. It's that thing you inherited; it's that thing that followed you whether you wanted it to or not.

Bloodline issues do not resolve through willpower alone. They require recognition. You cannot address what you refuse to name. This is also where the subject of evil covenants enters. Not every covenant made in a bloodline reflects God's heart. Let's face it, some are flat out evil.

Some were made: In famine, in fear, in captivity, in desperation, or under threat. Some were made by people who were just trying to survive. And survival covenants can outlive their usefulness—and their safety.

Scripture does not deny this reality; it records it. But Scripture also shows that covenants can be confronted, renounced, or:

- Redeemed

- Overruled

- Fulfilled differently

This can be accomplished even through one person willing to stand awake in the line: an intercessor. This is why redemption does not bypass bloodlines. It enters them.

Jesus is not traced back for sentiment. He is traced back for legitimacy, for authority. Bloodline establishes the right to rule.

If blood were irrelevant, lineage would not matter.

If covenants were symbolic, thrones would not require them.

God redeems *through* blood—not around it.

This chapter is not meant to make you fearful of where you come from. It is meant to make you see that you are standing in a line. That line carries both gifts and burdens. Ignoring either is not freedom. Stewarding both is Wisdom.

Blood is covenantal, not merely biological

WHY GOD THINKS IN LINES

Modern thinking is individual-centered. We are taught to see people as isolated decision-makers, self-defining units, free to reinvent themselves at will. Success and failure are framed as personal. Identity is framed as chosen. Responsibility is framed as optional. That is not true; Scripture does not reason this way.

God thinks in **lines**.

From the opening chapters of Genesis onward, God addresses humanity through houses, families, generations, nations; and through tribes. Even when He speaks to individuals, He speaks *through* them. Even when only one person is addressed, an entire line is affected.

This is why Scripture rarely introduces someone without telling you *where they come from*. This is not because God is nostalgic; it is because origin determines jurisdiction. *Where you come from answers questions such as What you are authorized to confront? What follows you without invitation? What responds when you speak? What resists when you move?*

God does not correct problems only at the surface. He addresses sources. Lines are sources. This is why God makes promises that outlive the person who receives them.

He does not say: **I will bless you for your lifetime**. He says: **I will bless your descendants**. God names how many generations. He told David that one of his descendants would always be on the throne. In blessing, I will bless you and in multiplying, I will multiply you. That is line-thinking. It is also why Scripture shows generational consequences.

A line carries momentum.

This may be deeply uncomfortable for modern sensibilities, because it disrupts the idea that every battle is purely personal. Some battles are not about *you*. They are about where you come from. They are about where you stand. They are about where your **people** are going.

This also explains why God so often intervenes at transition points. He is at births, name changes, deaths, blessings, inheritances, and threshold moments. Those are moments where lines shift.

Consider how often God changes a name; a name change is not cosmetic; it is a line adjustment.

Abram becomes Abraham; Jacob becomes Israel.

God changes names because what flows through them is being altered. Jacob wrestles alone, but he emerges as a carrier of twelve tribes. The wrestling is personal. The outcome is generational. God sees the big picture always; He thinks in continuity. This is why God forgives and also restores, repairs, and reorders lines.

Redemption is not a reset button; It is a re-threading.

This is also why isolation is so dangerous spiritually. When people sever themselves from lines, from family, faith, or from accountability, they often believe they are protecting themselves. In reality, they are removing context. And without context, patterns go unnamed. When families dismiss one of the members, ignores them, skips over them or tries to push them out, they may be pushing away the very one that God sent to stand for that family line.

God's insistence on gathering is not about control; it is about preservation of the line. Lines require memory. Memory requires proximity. Proximity requires gathering. This is why "do not forsake the gathering" cannot be reduced to attendance. This requirement is a warning against disconnection from responsibility. When lines fragment, inheritance leaks. God thinks in lines because lines carry authority, lines carry responsibility.

Lines carry blessing. Lines carry repair. God may rescue isolated moments, but He is committed to redeeming history.

When God looks at you, He sees you and your BLOODLINE. Tribes have **blood** in common. There is responsibility to blood in the eyes of God (Am I my brother's keeper?). The New Testament also says, *do not forsake the gathering of yourselves together.* That means a lot of different things and not just about a church. How about a family? A bloodline? A tribe?

Blood, responsibility, and gathering—all three are connected to hold things together.

BLOOD CREATES
OBLIGATIONS *AND* PERMISSIONS

If the breath of God is "on loan," then the blood of man is not ours at all. Breath: Lent by God in Genesis 2:7, God breathes life into man. Breath comes from God. It sustains life. And it returns to God when life ends (cf. Ecclesiastes)

Breath is *granted*; it's borrowed life.

Blood is reserved by God. Scripture is even stricter about blood than it is about breath. In Leviticus 17:11, God says:

For the life of the flesh is in the blood, and I have given it to you upon the altar to make atonement...

Blood contains life. Life belongs to God. Blood is not for common use. It is set apart; it is holy, restricted, and governed.

In the Old Testament we will see that blood was forbidden for consumption. This is why murder was condemned so severely. All bloodshed required accounting. Blood is not on loan; it is under divine claim.

Breath is *lent* so life may function. With the Breath of God, man becomes a living soul.

Blood is *claimed* because life belongs to God.

You breathe because God allows it.

You do not own life itself. In Him, we move and breathe, and have being. Scripture treats blood as sacred, dangerous, and non-negotiable. Humans steward breath; we do not own life.

And, most importantly: we cannot traffic in blood without consequence.

Only God has jurisdiction over when life begins, and when life ends, and how life is redeemed. That is why redemption ultimately required blood, not borrowed from man, but offered by Christ — life given back to God by God Himself.

Breath sustains life, but blood belongs to God.

This cuts straight to jurisdiction; Scripture fiercely guards the difference between what is stewarded versus what is owned.

This explains why violence is never casual in Scripture, and why blood guilt cries out. Everything God makes is alive; therefore, blood can cry out because it is not dead and never dies. We may think blood gets old, it dries up – not to God. It is blood and it is still speaking, testifying, and God hears it.

The sacredness of blood also explains why sacrifice required blood. And it tells us why redemption could never be transactional or symbolic only.

You can steward what is lent.

You cannot trade what is claimed. It is not yours to sell or to trade. That's why attempts to own people, souls, obedience, conscience, or life itself always cross into illegality. They trespass into God's reserved domain.

God does not see you in isolation — He sees you *and* your bloodline. When God looks at a person in Scripture, He is never looking at a single dot. Just as you and many others have wondered, *Do I belong? Where do I fit in? Who do I look like? God is checking you for fit too. Who is this one? Where does he or she belong?* God sees origins, lines covenants, Blessings and breaches. He sees promises still in transit. This is why Scripture is saturated with genealogies; yes, God loves records. But it is because blood carries responsibility.

"Am I my brother's keeper?" was not a casual question. It was an attempted escape from blood responsibility; but it didn't work.

The implied Biblical answer is: Yes. You are your brother's keeper and he is yours, also. Blood is not merely biological in Scripture. It is relational, legal, and spiritual.

That's why blessings pass through bloodlines. Consequences echo through generations. Restoration often comes *through one person* willing to stand in the gap. A tribe, then, is not just people you like, **it is people whose outcomes are tied to yours.**

Tribes have blood in common, and blood creates obligation. Modern culture treats blood like trivia. Scripture treats blood like testimony.

Blood means:

- *I cannot pretend your fate does not affect mine*

- *Your fall diminishes us*

- *Your healing strengthens us*

- *Your inheritance is connected to my obedience*

Real tribal thinking demands responsibility without romance. A clique can walk away. A trauma bond can dissolve. A tribe must reckon. Blood makes demands. Blood asks questions. Blood requires answers.

Blood creates obligations (and permissions) Covenants. There may be evil covenants that your people made that need to be broken. If God went thru the process of tracing Jesus from Abraham, and that a man from David's bloodline would always be on the Throne then we can see the importance of blood and lineage. In Scripture, blood is never neutral.

Blood establishes:

- **Obligations** (what you are responsible for)

- **Permissions** (what you are authorized to access)

- **Restrictions** (what follows you until addressed)

What covenants are governing you because of the tribe you came from? Do you even know what they are?

WHAT WAS SIGNED BEFORE YOU WERE BORN?

Before you made choices, choices were already shaping the conditions you entered. Not spiritually spooky—jurisdictionally real.

This chapter is about agreements, obligations, and permissions that predated personal consent.

Not everything that affects you began with you. Many of us have asked, "Who signed my name?" This book helps us ask a steadier question: *What covenants were already in motion when I arrived?* You inherit conditions. You inherit expectations. You inherit permissions and limits. You inherit situations and also consequences.

None of that means guilt; it means context.

You were born into a story already in motion.

What "was signed" can mean vows, oaths, covenants, alliances, decisions made under pressure, survival agreements, cultural or family rules that were never questioned.

Some were spoken. Some were silent. Some were practical. Some were desperate. All of them had jurisdictional weight.

Why do these agreements still matter? Because agreements create obligations, expectations, boundaries, permissions, and prohibitions

Those don't expire just because generations pass. You meet them where they are:

"Why do I feel resistance I didn't choose?"
"Why do the same patterns keep repeating?"
"Why does leaving feel harder than it should?"

Answered plainly: *Because some things were never renegotiated.*

As said, this is not about ancestral *spirits,* mystical contracts, hidden rituals, fear-based genealogy. This is about governance, not ghosts.

Authority can review what you never agreed to. You don't need to know who signed, what year, what tribe, what land. You only need to know who outranks it. The only Person who outranks it all is Jesus Christ. *Christ does not require your understanding to exercise His authority.*

Father God,
I bring before You anything that touched my life
before I had a voice.
Where agreements were made without my consent,
where obligations still speak,
where expectations limit what You have called me
to—
I place all of it under Your authority.
I receive only what comes from You,
and I release what does not.
Amen.

Small prayer: big impact. Very effective.

You are not responsible for what was signed
before you were born, but you are authorized to place
it under rightful authority now because you are in that
tribe and you have jurisdiction within it.

The parents eat sour grapes,
and the children's teeth are set on edge.

(Ezekiel 18 and Jeremiah 31)

This proverb describes inherited effect without
personal cause. Someone before you made a choice.
They absorbed the taste. You feel the consequence.
You didn't eat the grapes. But your teeth ache anyway.
That's jurisdictional language.

God is saying, (paraphrased), *"Stop using this
proverb as an excuse."* because He is changing the
rules of accountability. He's saying, **Yes**, patterns pass

44

down. Consequences linger; but you are not trapped by them forever. Each person can now stand directly accountable to God, not only to inherited outcomes.

The sour grapes were real. The teeth-on-edge experience is real. But the proverb is not the final word; The final word is: Authority can intervene in inheritance.

Ezekiel 18 doesn't deny inherited impact. It denies inherited inevitability. So, the message becomes: You may feel what you didn't choose. You may carry what you didn't cause. But you are not forbidden from placing it under God's authority.

That's not rebellion against or disrespect toward your parents.That's alignment with God. *The Bible acknowledges inherited consequences—but it refuses inherited hopelessness. Sour grapes explain the ache. Authority explains the cure.*

You're not stuck. In Christ, none of us are stuck.

Scripture acknowledges inherited consequences, but it promises that they no longer have final authority over those who stand under God's covenant. The ache may be inherited, but the outcome is not. There is much good in Christ; some of it needs to be declared, else, there are forces that would try to withhold it from you.

INHERITED COVENANTS

A covenant is an agreement that establishes terms of relationship. In Scripture, covenants govern access, authority, protection, consequence and continuity. They determine what is allowed, what is forbidden, and what must be answered.

The modern mistake is assuming that a covenant only applies to the person who made it.

Biblically, that is rarely true. Covenants attach to lines (bloodlines).

This is why Scripture records covenants so carefully—who made them, under what conditions, and with what consequences. A covenant does not dissolve simply because time passes or because the original parties are gone.

Covenants persist until they are fulfilled, broken, replaced, redeemed or overruled by a greater covenant.

Many people are governed by covenants they never consciously chose, because they were born into jurisdiction.

Inheritance precedes consent. Some inherited covenants are holy. They bring favor, preservation, Wisdom, stability, and blessing that feels "unearned."

These covenants often appear as doors opening without explanation. Protection that shows up repeatedly. Grace that precedes effort. This is not luck; it is covenantal momentum.

Other inherited covenants are mixed. They include blessing *and* limitation. They may have both provision *and* dysfunction. One may see strength paired with recurring struggle. These are the most confusing, because they make life feel inconsistent. If a covenant was made with the dark kingdom, there is a dark consequence on one side while the person who made the deal got something 'good' that they wanted, needed or desired. That is the nature of evil covenants. The devil's trades are evil and there will be evil in that covenant somewhere whether it is obvious and known or if it is hidden in very fine print.

Something works. Something doesn't. Something repeats. And then there are covenants that are destructive. These are not theoretical.

Scripture shows covenants made with false gods, In times of fear, Under threat, During famine or siege,

Through bloodshed, vows, or compromise. These covenants were often made to survive a moment. But survival covenants can bind generations. An evil covenant does not announce itself as evil.

It often presents as "This is how our family survives." "This is just how we are." "Everyone in our line struggles with this." "This has always been the cost."

Normalization is how covenantal damage hides. This is why repentance in Scripture is often corporate, not just individual. A king repents for a people. A leader repents for a house. One person stands in the gap for a line. God addresses covenants through representatives.

Inherited covenants are not addressed by denial. They are addressed by recognition, Truth, or alignment with a higher covenant.

You cannot renounce what you refuse to acknowledge. This is also why prayer sometimes feels ineffective until language changes. General prayers ask for relief. Covenantal prayers ask for jurisdictional change.

They sound different.

Jesus does not erase covenants by ignoring them. He fulfills, confronts, and replaces them. This is why His blood is called a *new covenant*. It is legal language, real talk--, the Truth anyhow. A new covenant does not deny the old, it supersedes it. In Jesus' case, He fulfills the old covenant. Which means that old permissions are revoked. Old accusations lose standing. Old claims are answered, but only where the New Covenant is applied.

Many Believers live saved lives under unexamined inherited agreements if they have not exercised their discernment to spiritually map or look into these ancient or tribal agreements. You are not required to obsess over your bloodline. But you are responsible to steward what you are shown.

God reveals covenants when He intends to resolve them. Understanding inherited covenants does not trap you in the past. It positions you to end something, and end it properly. God is the Last; He is Omega; He knows very well how to end things and that is one of His favorite forms of Mercy.

Covenants govern whole bloodlines, not just individuals. Inheritance precedes consent; if it is in your bloodline, you will inherit it. Period. If it's good; then bless the Lord. If it's bad and you don't inherit it, bless the Lord, because it was only by His Mercy that it didn't pass to you. But now you can understand how certain diseases, for example, skip generations. It's in the bloodline but the Mercy of God caused it to skip you.

Prayer for My Tribe.
It assumes uncertainty, guards against presumption,
and deals explicitly with **unknown and inherited
covenants**—without fear or theatrics.

PRAYER FOR MY TRIBE

God Most High,
Creator of families, bloodlines, and nations—
I come to You asking for **clarity, covering, and
correction**.

Before I name a tribe,
before I align,
before I claim belonging,
I submit myself to **Your authority alone**.

If there are covenants attached to my bloodline
that I do not know,
that were made without my consent,
that were entered into through fear, survival,
ignorance, or sin—
I bring them now under the judgment of Christ.

I renounce every covenant
that did not originate in You,
every agreement that trades life for survival,
every oath that binds through blood but not
through righteousness.

Where my people made vows under pressure,
where promises were made to false *gods*,
systems, or powers,

where survival replaced obedience—
I ask that those covenants be **identified, judged,
and broken**
by the authority of the New Covenant in Christ.

I declare that no covenant
has greater authority than the Blood of Jesus.

If there are permissions operating in my life
because of lineage and not calling,
because of inheritance and not obedience,
I revoke them now where they oppose Your will.

If there are obligations assigned to my line
that You did not authorize,
I lay them down.

If there are blessings You intended
that have been delayed because of confusion,
silence, or fear,
I receive them now with humility and
discernment.

Lord, guard me from false belonging.
Guard me from adopting identity prematurely.
Guard me from entering alliances
that look like family but carry hidden bondage.

If my tribe is not yet fully revealed,
keep me protected while I wait.

If my tribe is fractured,
heal what You intend to heal
and separate what You intend to separate.

If my tribe carries history I am not yet ready to
face,
give me Wisdom before exposure
and covering before confrontation.

I ask not to be cut off from my people,
but to be rightly aligned within them.

Let me recognize my tribe
not by emotion,
not by trauma,
not by shared wounds or shared enemies,
but by **truth, covenant, and responsibility**.

And until clarity is given,
I choose obedience over curiosity,
discernment over assumption,
and rest over striving.

I stand under the authority of Christ alone.
I belong to You before I belong anywhere else.

**Thank You, Lord for answered prayer. In the
Name of Jesus, Amen.**

PERMISSIONS YOU DIDN'T APPLY FOR

Not all authority is earned; some authority is **inherited**. It is inherited by your parentage, your bloodline, your tribe, your ethnicity, your culture, your nation. Some authority is inherited just by being born a human being in the Earth realm.

Many people assume that if they did not consciously choose something, it cannot have jurisdiction over them. Scripture does not support that assumption.

Jurisdiction often precedes awareness.

Permissions are the unseen counterpart to obligations. If obligations tell you what you are responsible for, permissions tell you what you are allowed to touch, confront, enter, or influence. Some permissions come through obedience. Others come through assignment, and some come through bloodline.

This is why certain people encounter resistance in places where others move freely—and why some people move with ease where others struggle. It is not favoritism; it is **jurisdiction**.

Inherited permissions can appear as authority in particular spaces. It can appear as discernment around specific issues, access to influence without striving, or an unusual ability to confront certain patterns. Some may see doors that open repeatedly in one area and not another. These *permissions* often feel "natural," which is why they are overlooked. What is inherited rarely announces itself.

The opposite is also true.

There are boundaries you may encounter—not because you lack faith or effort—but because the permission has not been granted. Trying to cross those boundaries through force leads to exhaustion, not breakthrough.

Authority cannot be faked.

This is why comparison is so destructive. When you envy another person's results, you are often envying **their** *permissions*, not their effort. Permissions cannot be lent or borrowed. Bloodline permissions explain why some battles respond when *you* speak—but not when someone else does.

This also explains why some battles ignore you entirely. This is not failure. It is information.

Scripture repeatedly shows God sending people to confront issues that match their line. Moses is sent back to Egypt. David confronts giants. Prophets speak to kings. Priests deal with defilement.

Assignment follows jurisdiction.

This is also why people sometimes feel compelled to address issues that others avoid. They sense responsibility where others feel none. That sense is not random.

Inherited permissions are not rewards. They are **tools,** and tools come with accountability. If you have authority in an area, you will also face resistance there.

Permission and pressure often travel together.

Some people misuse the idea of permission to justify passivity *"I guess this isn't my assignment."* Others misuse it to justify overreach *"I'm called to everything."* Both are incorrect interpretations of jurisdiction.

True authority is quiet. It does not announce itself. It does not compete. It does not explain itself endlessly. It simply **functions**.

Understanding your permissions helps you stay in your lane—not out of limitation, but out of effectiveness. When you speak where you are authorized, things shift. When you speak outside your jurisdiction, things collapse right then and again and again in the echo.

This chapter is not asking you to seek more power. It is asking you to recognize the power you already carry—and to use it responsibly. Some permissions were not earned by you. They were **entrusted** to you. What you do with them matters.

Authority often precedes awareness. Permission explains both ease and resistance. Woe unto those who are at ease in Zion; so do as you are instructed and empowered.

WHEN EVIL COVENANTS GO UNNAMED

Not every covenant operating in a bloodline is holy. This statement does not require fear. It requires honesty. Scripture records covenants that brought life—and covenants that brought harm. Some were made with God. Others were made in desperation, ignorance, fear, or rebellion.

A covenant does not need to be righteous to be effective. It only needs to be recognized by the parties involved. Evil covenants rarely announce themselves as evil. They hide behind language like:

- "This is how we survive."

- "This is the cost of being who we are."

- "This is just our family."

- "Every generation deals with this."

When something destructive is normalized, it stops being questioned. Many harmful covenants were formed during famine, war, captivity, slavery, exile, systemic injustice, personal trauma or other points of desperation.

They were often survival decisions, not moral ones. Survival covenants can outlive the crisis that produced them.

This is why some patterns repeat even when the original conditions no longer exist.

The famine is gone. The captivity is over. The threat has passed. But the agreement remains. An unexamined covenant continues by default. Silence does not neutralize it. Time does not weaken it. Ignorance does not dissolve it; only **truth** does.

This is where many people become uncomfortable—because naming something inherited feels like accusation. But Scripture does not treat recognition as blame. It treats it as **responsibility**. You are not held accountable for what your ancestors did not know. But you are responsible for what you **now see**.

This is why God often reveals these things slowly. Not to overwhelm—but to prepare. Exposure without authority creates fear. Authority without exposure creates stagnation. God times revelation carefully.

When evil covenants go unnamed, they manifest as repeating cycles, chronic patterns that resist prayer. They could show up as disproportionate resistance in specific areas. Familial strongholds that feel "normal." There could be a sense of limitation without clear cause. These are not proof of failure. They are signals of **jurisdictional conflict**. Scripture shows that covenants are addressed through confession. Renunciation. Alignment with a higher Covenant. Obedience that contradicts the old agreement. Not theatrics. Not obsession. Not fear, but Divine Order.

The Blood of Christ is not symbolic language. It is covenantal language. A new covenant does not erase history. It **answers it**.

Covenants must be invoked where they apply. Many believers know they are redeemed—but have never **applied** redemption to inherited agreements.

They pray for relief instead of resolution. Relief manages symptoms. Resolution changes jurisdiction. This chapter is not an invitation to hunt for demons or invent histories. It is an invitation to ask better questions. *What keeps repeating? What resists correction? What feels older than me? What survives every surface-level fix? Those questions are not dangerous; They are discerning.*

Evil covenants lose power when they are named—not because naming is magical, but because truth restores **order** which is one of God's primary weapons.

If something in your line has been operating unchallenged, it is not because God is indifferent. It may be because **you** are the one positioned to address it. Perhaps this is why you are the one designated to pray for your tribe, either with others, or because no one else is.

Unnamed covenants persist by default

Recognition precedes resolution

OTHER TRIBES

The Bible does not explicitly say that all non-Israelite tribes are pagan but we know that the 12 Tribes of Jacob are the structure for God's chosen people. Later in the New Testament God grafts in the Gentiles; so there is room in the Kingdom for all who will come. However, I have heard teaching that every festival is to some deity, so if it is not to God, then to *whom*? The Bible does teach us clearly that no tribe or the deities they serve, anywhere, has the power of Salvation; only in Christ are we saved. No culture mediates God. No ritual replaces covenant obedience.

Every people group has history, culture, has customs, and memory.

But we know that only one Covenant redeems.

The issue is not *having* a tribe; the issue is what authority that tribe claims over the person now.

Christ does not erase ethnicity or culture. He does reassign ultimate allegiance. Once saved, we state who has lordship over our lives from then on.

Any demand that contradicts their allegiance to Christ is idolatrous and God hates idolatry.

If you are part of an ancestral tribe that insists on rituals or festivals, here's the governing principle: Participation becomes a problem when it requires submission, invocation, or spiritual allegiance.

So, we must distinguish between cultural participation, which may be permissible, from something required that is more than surface, or there is some other worship hidden in the practice itself. Is a family gathering simply a family gathering? Or, is it something else? Is it a renewal of covenants--, even covenants that you didn't even know were in place? Is the food simply food, or has it been dedicated to idols? Is the music just music? The storytelling, the memory, the history—is it completely innocent or is it an initiation, a dedication, or a renewal?

Spiritual submission is not permissible if you are in Christ and know and believe that you are. Invoking other *gods* or *spirits* is not acceptable. Ritual sacrifice, oath-making, ancestral mediation and acts explicitly framed as worship or appeasement are not at all permissible.

The New Testament already dealt with this issue (meat offered to idols, festival participation, family pressure). The answer was not panic—it was discernment and conscience.

A Believer may say:

- "I can attend, but I will not invoke."

- "I can observe, but I will not submit."

- "I can honor people, but not powers."

Sometimes *presence* is all that is required to rope a person in or back into something they left months or years ago. The believer may need to decline participation, calmly and respectfully. That is not rebellion. That is maintaining alignment with God.

When you surrender to idols, dethroning Christ you are also setting down your authority in Christ. There is no authority in Christ outside of Christ. So now when you need the Lord, to witness, speak, pray, heal, be blessed or blessed others, where is your power and authority?

Is it back at the festival, where you laid it down, and now you're powerless?

Being in Christ does not require rejecting your people, but it does require rejecting any claim of authority that rivals Christ. It requires you to deny worship to any entity, deity, spirit or power that is requiring worship of you. That includes ancestral demands, tribal expectations, cultural pressure, and family insistence. Your momma may cry and your dad may threaten to disown you, but neither of them have a Heaven or Hell to put you in—no disrespect intended.

Christ doesn't ask people to become culture-less. He asks them to become governed.

I am not telling anyone to shun their people or to replace their ethnicity with Israel. I'm telling no one to denounce their history. I am providing facts and you must govern yourself accordingly.

Perhaps these questions are useful:

- *What covenants claim authority over me?*

- *Which ones am I still submitting to without realizing it?*

- *Where does Christ sit in that order?*

AM I MY BROTHER'S KEEPER?

The first question asked after the first murder in Scripture is not about violence. It is about responsibility. *"Am I my brother's keeper?"* is not a philosophical inquiry. It is a legal deflection. Cain is not asking for clarity, he is attempting to narrow jurisdiction.

In essence, he is saying, *"Is this really my responsibility?"*

God's response makes it clear that blood creates obligation whether one accepts it or not.

Responsibility did not begin with consent. It began with relationship.

Modern culture is deeply uncomfortable with this idea. We are taught to draw boundaries quickly, to disengage easily, and to measure responsibility by personal choice. Scripture measures responsibility by proximity and blood.

Not every responsibility is equal. But blood responsibility is never zero.

This does not mean enabling harm. It does not mean tolerating abuse. It does not mean refusing Wisdom. It means recognizing that detachment does not erase consequence. When someone in a bloodline falters, the line is affected.

Not because everyone shares guilt, but because everyone shares impact. This is why Scripture shows families suffering for the actions of one. Households being restored through the obedience of one. Tribes rising or falling together.

Responsibility in Scripture is not about control; it is about custodianship. A keeper does not own what they guard. They steward it. This is why God often calls people to stand in the gap. Standing in the gap does not mean absorbing blame; it means interrupting a trajectory.

Some people refuse responsibility because they fear being overwhelmed. Others refuse it because they fear being inconvenienced.

Both miss the point. Responsibility does not mean carrying everything. It means carrying what is assigned.

This is where discernment matters.

Not every burden is yours But some burdens *are*, simply because of where you stand in the line. Ignoring them does not make them disappear. It often makes them louder.

This is also why Scripture places such emphasis on firstborns, elders, and heads of households. These roles are not honorary. They are load bearing.

Being a keeper does not mean fixing people. It means refusing to pretend that what happens to them has nothing to do with you. In modern language, we often replace responsibility with sympathy. Sympathy feels compassionate, but it carries no obligation.

A keeper does more than feel. A keeper acts within jurisdiction. This chapter is not asking you to take on what you cannot carry. It is asking you to stop pretending that blood carries no weight. If you belong to a line, you are already implicated. The only question is whether you will be conscious or unconscious in that role.

God does not ask Cain if he loved his brother. He asks where his brother is. Responsibility begins there. Blood creates responsibility regardless of consent

DO NOT FORSAKE THE GATHERING

The instruction *"Do not forsake the gathering of yourselves together"* has been narrowed over time. It is often treated as a rule about attendance—show up, be present, occupy a seat. *Do not forsake the gathering* is larger than church attendance; that New Testament instruction has been flattened. "Do not forsake the gathering of yourselves together" is not merely a command to attend a service or a seating chart in a sanctuary; it is a pattern of preservation.

That gathering may be a literal family you must engage with wisely. It could be a bloodline that needs prayerful repair. Maybe it's a tribe that must be re-formed, not replaced. Or, it could be a household of faith that functions like kin. The warning isn't about absence; It's about disintegration.

Isolation fractures inheritance.

But Scripture is rarely concerned with presence without connection. The warning is not about missing a meeting. It is about breaking continuity.

Gathering, in Scripture, is a safeguard. It preserves memory, accountability, correction, transmission, and inheritance. When gathering breaks down, lines weaken. God does not command gathering to manage behavior. He commands it to prevent fragmentation.

Isolation is not neutral.

It alters outcomes.

Gathering in Scripture includes more than formal worship. It includes families, households, elders, kin, tribes, and covenant communities. *Do not live disconnected from the people to whom you owe responsibility.*

These are places where stories are told, patterns are recognized, blessings are spoken, errors are corrected, responsibilities are named. When people forsake gathering, they often believe they are protecting themselves. Sometimes they are. But often, they are unintentionally cutting themselves off from context. Context reveals patterns. Without context, repetition feels personal instead of inherited. This is why God repeatedly regathers people.

For example, after exile, after rebellion, and after dispersion, God will gather the people together.

Gathering is God's response to scattering. Scattering produces confusion. Gathering produces clarity.

This does not mean every gathering is healthy. Scripture also warns against assemblies that reinforce error. Not all gatherings preserve life. Some preserve dysfunction. Some renew covenants and every covenant is not good. Discernment matters.

Abandoning gathering altogether is not the answer. God does not heal lines through isolation. He heals them through re-formation. This is also why gathering carries responsibility. When you gather, you become visible. When you become visible, patterns can be addressed.

Isolation hides patterns. Gathering exposes them—not to shame, but to resolve. This chapter is not calling you to return to places that harmed you. It is calling you to understand why disconnection alone rarely produces freedom. Freedom requires witness, accountability, memory, and continuity. These require proximity.

A tribe gathers not because everyone agrees, but because what happens to one affects the rest. Gathering is not comfort; it is commitment.

This is why Scripture treats persistent isolation as dangerous, unless, of course, God called a person to solitude for a season and for His own reasons. Not because God fears independence, but because inheritance cannot be carried alone. *Do not forsake the gathering* is not a threat, it is a protection.

It means: Do not sever yourself from the people who help you see clearly who you are, where you come from, and what you are responsible for.

Gathering keeps the line intact. Gathering preserves continuity, not attendance

Isolation alters inheritance

Even if you cannot connect in the same place or space with your tribe, if you even know who they are--, pray for your tribe.

FAMILY, BLOODLINE, TRIBE

The words, *family*, *bloodline*, and *tribe* are often used interchangeably. Scripture does not treat them as the same thing. They are related, but they are not identical. Understanding the distinction matters because confusion here creates misplaced expectations and unnecessary strain.

Family, bloodline, tribe are different expressions of the same call. Family is the immediate expression of blood responsibility. Bloodline is the generational extension of that responsibility. Tribe is the organized, accountable structure that *carries* that responsibility forward.

A tribe is what forms when blood is acknowledged, responsibility is accepted, gathering is maintained, correction is allowed, and memory is preserved.

This is why Scripture doesn't celebrate lone spiritual heroes as much as it tracks *houses*. God does not just heal individuals. He repairs lines.

This means your obedience may not be primarily for you. Your clarity may stabilize people you will never meet. Your refusal to disengage may interrupt cycles older than you. Gathering protects inheritance—, not just attendance. That's tribal responsibility. That's bloodline stewardship. That's why gathering matters.

God does not save in fragments. He redeems people in lines.

This book is not asking people to romanticize ancestry. It's inviting them to re-enter responsibility with Wisdom.

Family is the most immediate expression of relationship. Family is where life begins. It is personal, close, and formative. Family shapes early identity, emotional language, relational patterns. First experiences of authority and care. Family is where love is learned—or distorted.

Bloodline is broader. A bloodline is not just who raised you, it is also, who came before you—and who comes after. Bloodline carries history, memory, blessings and breaches, repeated patterns, and long arcs of consequence. You may know your family well and know very little about your bloodline.

But the bloodline still operates.

Tribe is the structured expression of responsibility that emerges when family and bloodline are recognized and ordered. A tribe is not merely related people. It is related people who accept mutual obligation.

Tribe is where responsibility becomes organized.

Family is personal. Bloodline is generational. Tribe is covenantal. This is why tribes in Scripture had elders, laws, boundaries, inheritance rules, and accountability structures. A tribe exists to carry a line forward intact. When family fractures, bloodline does not disappear, but when bloodline goes unrecognized, tribe weakens. When tribe collapses, inheritance leaks. These are not emotional outcomes. They are structural ones.

Modern culture often tries to replace tribe with *chosen family*. Chosen relationships can be meaningful. They can even be healing. But chosen family does not automatically carry bloodline authority.

Substitution without discernment creates confusion. This does not mean people are trapped by biology. Scripture allows for adoption, grafting, covenant inclusion, new lineage through obedience. But even these processes are formal. They are not casual.

They involve recognition and responsibility, not just affection. A tribe forms where blood is acknowledged, history is told truthfully, responsibility is accepted, authority is respected, and continuity is protected. Without these elements, a group may be supportive—but it is not a tribe. This is also why tribes are uncomfortable. They remember what individuals would prefer to forget. They hold people to account across time. They refuse to let patterns reset every generation.

Family asks, *"How are you?"* Bloodline asks, *"What keeps repeating?"* Tribe asks, *"Who is responsible to address this?"* Understanding these distinctions relieves pressure. You do not expect your family to function as a tribe if the structure is not there. You do not expect chosen relationships to carry inherited jurisdiction they were never meant to hold. You do not blame yourself for outcomes that belong to a broader line.

Confusion between family, bloodline, and tribe causes misplaced guilt, false expectations, and unnecessary conflict.

Clarity restores Peace.

You belong to a family. You stand in a bloodline. You are accountable to a tribe, whether fully formed or not. Recognizing which is which allows you to move wisely. A tribe does not replace family or erase bloodline. It orders them.

TRIBAL JURISDICTION

When (especially) African pastors (and others) say things like:

- *"Your tribe is calling you back"*
- *"Your people won't let you leave"*
- *"That's why life is hard away from home"*

They are describing a lived experience, but often using shorthand language. They're pointing to unresolved authority structures and inherited obligations that were never named, broken, or superseded. In other words, jurisdiction that was never formally released.

What *is* the "jurisdiction of your tribe," really? The jurisdiction of your tribe is the set of obligations, expectations, permissions, and prohibitions that were assigned to your line—whether you agreed to them or not.

It's not a place. It's not a *spirit*. It's not even always conscious, but it is a governing pattern.

These assignments could have been made hundreds of years ago, but they are still affecting your tribe. Not only that, you may not be in touch with your tribe or even know who or where they are, but the spiritual issues of that tribe are affecting your life.

You feel the pressure. You may not have a name for it, but you've tried everything, prayed everything and these perceived pressures have not let up.

Have you prayed for your tribe? Have you done warfare for your tribe and to shut down any evil covenants that are still warring against you because you are not submitting to them and you don't even know what they are? You don't even know that they exist. You probably wouldn't know hot to fulfill them if you could. And, if you are in Christ, you don't even want to try to fulfill them because you want to keep Jesus on the throne of your heart.

What if you don't know who the tribe is or where it is? Then we are not talking about geography. We are talking about inheritance without a name.

Many people don't know the tribe, don't know the land, don't know the language and don't know the customs. But they still experience guilt when they leave, a tug to go back--, go back where? They notice sabotage when they advance or try to advance in life and they haven't been able to figure it out. They notice difficulty thriving elsewhere. And many are stuck in repeated cycles that don't match their effort.

So, the question becomes *What claims authority over me even when I'm not choosing it?*

That's jurisdiction.

Going *back* feels powerful for some people. When someone returns "home," a few things often happen automatically. Expectations reassert themselves. Roles snap back into place. Guilt quiets down. Pressure eases. Resistance lifts, although temporarily.

These things don't happen because the tribe is magical—but because the person is back inside the **system** that shaped them. That doesn't mean the system is good. It just means it's *familiar*.

Leaving a tribe, family system, or inherited structure often can feel hard, even when it's right. First there may be resistance from family and community. There could be jealousy – *Who do you think you are? Get off your high horse.* There may be fear in the person leaving; they may feel alone and unsure. The others may have vowed not to help them, threatening, *If you leave, don't ask me for anything.* They may have a fear of disappointing others, or even failing, but they know they should leave. It's the right thing for their life.

That creates friction, not because you're wrong, but because jurisdiction is being contested. The tribal jurisdiction does not want you to go.

I talk about his in my book **What Do You Have to Declare?** It is mostly about territorial *spirits* who want to own you, where you are, or wherever you go. Territorial *spirits* are what try to keep a person in one place all their lives. This is not the same as being established by the Lord, it is being stuck in one place even if you want to obey God and leave.

Unexamined inheritance can exert pressure even after physical separation. Know this: Christ outranks every inherited jurisdiction—named or unnamed.

So even if the tribe is unknown, you will notice patterns, permissions, limits, expectations, and obligations that predate the individual. This is because there are covenants, and unless you break a covenant, it lasts forever, and these covenants are governing that tribe and the members in it.

Even when a tribe is unknown, its jurisdiction may still be felt through inherited obligations—and those obligations can be placed under Christ's authority without ever naming the tribe.

So, recognize spiritual pressure, name the authority that is ruling. Submit what you don't understand to God. Don't blame yourself for inherited weight—there is no way it is your fault.

No matter who your tribe is or where it is, the question is: *"What is governing you?"* That question works even when the map is missing.

THE SCATTERED TRIBE

What if your Tribe has been scattered? How do you handle that? First: Scattering is not failure. In Scripture, scattering happens for many reasons and under many different scenarios. War, famine, exile, slavery and persecution, to name a few. Our God is merciful, sometimes there is scattering for our own protection and preservation.

Only God perfectly balances judgment and Mercy. Scattering is not always punishment; sometimes it's how a line **survives**.

If someone's tribe has been scattered, the first thing to remove is shame.

Scattering does not erase inheritance. It complicates continuity—but it does not nullify covenant.

A scattered tribe is a people whose land was lost. Their records were broken. Their names were altered. Their continuity was interrupted. Their authority structures collapsed. This resulted in a people who don't know where they're from. People who, even without a map, feel spiritual pressure. They inherit unknown patterns without explanations. They carry weights they didn't choose.

This is incredibly common, especially among descendants of slavery, refugees, war-displaced families, colonized peoples, and families fractured by addiction, poverty, or violence. (There is no people group on the entire Earth who have not been enslaved by some other group at some time or other throughout history. Some people groups were enslaved by their own people.)

Be of good faith: God does not lose track of what history scatters. People lose records. God does not. People distort records; God does not. People destroy records; God does not. So, the scattered tribe is not invisible to Him, even if it's invisible to itself.

When the tribe is scattered, do not pray to find the tribe. Instead, pray to place what is unknown under God's authority.

Acknowledge scattering. "Father, my people have been scattered. I don't know the names, places, or paths—but You do. Every covenant ratified or endorsed by the tribe that my people and my bloodline hail from that is not of You, for You, from You, like You and that serves You, I break that covenant by the power in the Blood of Jesus and I submit it to Your Divine Authority in Jesus' Name. Amen."

Submit inherited obligations you didn't choose

"Lord, where obligations, expectations, or covenants touched my line without my consent, I place them under Your authority, in the Name of Jesus."

This is jurisdictional prayer.

Renounce illegitimate claims. Even if you don't know what the claims against you are; renounce them. "Father, I release any claim over my life that does not come from You, whether named or unnamed, remembered or forgotten, in the Name of Jesus."

Receive legitimate inheritance in Christ.

"Father, I receive what You have preserved for my line through Christ—identity, freedom, and rightful belonging, in the Name of Jesus."

Ask for governance, not reunion. Don't ask to go back. Don't ask to reconstruct the past. Ask, "Lord, teach me how to live rightly now, with what You've entrusted to me, in Jesus' Name."

Pray, but don't just pray. For the scattered tribe, the work is usually building healthy continuity forward. Ending patterns here. Work with what you have. Become a wise stewarding of what remains. Refuse false substitutes for *belonging.* In other words, don't try to rebuild the tribe backward like a retrofit. Instead, govern the line forward. That's how scattering is redeemed.

Scattered does not always mean judged or cursed. Abraham went one way and Lot went the other way. Scattered does not always mean incomplete, powerless or abandoned.

It can mean preserved through dispersion. Protected by anonymity. Freed from oppressive structures. Positioned for new stewardship.

Some tribes were not destroyed, they were scattered. Scattering breaks continuity, obscures names, and erases maps, but it does not erase God's knowledge or authority. Those who come from scattered lines are not required to reconstruct what history has broken. They are invited to place what is unknown under God's jurisdiction and to govern their lives forward in Christ.

When a tribe is scattered, the prayer is not for recovery of the past, but for rightful governance in the present.

BLOODLINES MATTER

If bloodlines did not matter, Jesus would not have a genealogy. Scripture could have begun the story of Christ with power alone—miracles, authority, Heaven opening, angels announcing. Instead, it pauses to trace a line. Not once, but twice. Genealogy is not ornamentation. It is legitimacy. A throne is never claimed by power alone. It is claimed by right. This is why kings are not simply strong men. They are men who stand in recognized lines.

Jesus is introduced not just as Savior, but as heir. He is traced to Abraham—the covenant of promise. He is traced to David—the covenant of kingship. These are not poetic choices; they are legal ones. God did not redeem humanity by bypassing lineage.

He entered it. He submitted Himself to bloodline, history, covenant, and consequence. That is not weakness. That is authority expressed correctly.

Jesus did not appear detached from history. He appeared answering it. Every promise, every breach, every expectation tied to those lines converged in Him. This is why Scripture insists that a man from David's bloodline would always sit on the throne. The throne is covenantal. The bloodline establishes jurisdiction.

This also explains why Jesus' genealogy includes people whose stories are uncomfortable. There are outsiders, scandals, broken decisions, compromised moments, and moral complexity. Redemption does not require a pristine line, but it does require an honest one.

God does not edit history to make redemption respectable. He redeems history as it is. Jesus' bloodline tells the truth about human failure, about covenant endurance, about God's refusal to abandon lines even when people falter. This matters deeply for anyone wrestling with inherited patterns. If God did not discard Christ's lineage because of its mess, He is not intimidated by yours.

The genealogy of Jesus settles a question many people ask quietly, *Does where I come from disqualify me?* The answer, in Christ, is no. But it also answers a harder question, *Does where I come from matter?* The answer is yes.

Jesus does not erase bloodlines; He fulfills them. He does not deny covenant.

He completes it. This is why the New Covenant is not abstract. It is sealed in Blood. It is sealed in Jurisdiction.

When you stand in Christ, you are not pretending your line never existed. You are standing in a greater covenant that has the authority to address every lesser one.

But authority must be applied.

Jesus' genealogy teaches us this: God does not rescue individuals by isolating them from history. He redeems lines by inserting Himself into them. If Christ was willing to enter lineage to redeem it, then lineage is not something to ignore. It is something to understand—so it can be answered.

Genealogy establishes legitimacy and jurisdiction. Redemption enters lineage; it does not bypass it

Genealogies matter because thrones require legitimacy. That's foundation.

This feels like arrival because the questions have stopped being searched and started being governed. You're no longer asking *"What could this be?"* You're asking, *"How does this operate?"* That shift means you've crossed the threshold. This is what I'm responsible for stewarding next.

FROM JACOB TO ISRAEL

Before there was a nation, there was a man. Before there was a tribe, there was a name. Jacob is not introduced in Scripture as a hero. He is introduced as a struggler, a schemer, a man trying to secure inheritance by effort rather than trust. And yet, Jacob is chosen.

Many people assume that tribal inheritance belongs only to the stable, the faithful, or the morally impressive. Scripture says otherwise. Inheritance often passes through people who are unfinished.

Jacob's story is not about morality first. It is about identity. Jacob spends much of his life striving for what was already promised. He grabs. He negotiates. He maneuvers, not because he is evil—but because he does not yet trust that inheritance can be received. This is why Jacob wrestles. Not in public. Not for show. Not for applause. He wrestles alone, at night, with no audience. The wrestling is not about victory or things and stuff. It is about name.

Jacob does not become Israel because he wins. He becomes Israel because he stays. He refuses to let go without transformation.

A name change in Scripture is never cosmetic. It marks a shift in authority, assignment, what flows through a person, and what they carry forward. Jacob becomes Israel not because his past is erased, but because his relationship to it changes. This is the pattern of tribal redemption. God does not remove Jacob from the line. He reorders the line through Jacob.

Twelve tribes emerge from a man who once lived in fear of loss. This is important for anyone wrestling with bloodline questions. You do not have to be perfect to be pivotal. You do not have to resolve everything in your line to be used to redirect it.

But you do have to wrestle honestly.

Jacob limps after the encounter. Transformation leaves a mark. Anyone who tells you that spiritual maturity leaves you untouched is not telling the truth. Change costs something. The limp is not weakness; it is memory. It reminds Jacob—and everyone after him—that blessing did not come from striving alone.

This is also why Israel's tribes carry complexity. They are not pristine. They are not uniform. They are not equally faithful. They are human. They are **named, a**nd naming brings order.

Many people want the inheritance of Israel without the wrestling of Jacob. They want authority without encounter. Blessing without confrontation. Continuity without surrender. Scripture does not offer that path.

Can you find yourself in Jacob?

Not the polished version or the anxious one. The grasping one. The one who knows something is promised—but is afraid it could be lost. If you can, then this chapter, this book offers hope. Because Jacob becomes Israel not by being replaced, but by being transformed **in place**. That is how lines are redeemed.

God does not need you to disown where you came from. He invites you to wrestle until you can carry it. Even if you carry it differently; you will still carry it.

Israel is not a personality upgrade. It is a **jurisdictional shift**. Jurisdiction shifts do not happen in crowds; they happen in encounters.

This chapter is not about striving harder. It is about staying present long enough for God to rename what you carry. Transformation reorders inheritance without erasing history. Naming follows wrestling, not performance.

STANDING IN THE GAP FOR A LINE

Every line reaches a moment where continuation alone is no longer enough. Something must be addressed, not just endured. This is where the language of *standing in the gap* becomes precise. Standing in the gap is not heroism; it is work. It is positioning.

It means recognizing that you are located at a point in a line where awareness has increased, language has clarified, authority has been recognized, and responsibility can no longer be deferred.

A gap exists when something has been broken, distorted, or left unresolved. Standing in the gap does not mean carrying guilt for the past. It means **interrupting negative momentum**. Scripture shows this pattern repeatedly one person repents on behalf of many. One person obeys where others compromised. One person names what others normalized. One person stands awake while others remain fully asleep or unaware.

This is not favoritism. It is assignment. Standing in the gap does not require perfection.

It requires honesty, discernment, courage to remain present, willingness to act without applause. Many people avoid this role because they misunderstand it. They assume standing in the gap means carrying everyone, fixing everything, absorbing endless responsibility. Scripture does not support that.

Standing in the gap means acting within jurisdiction. You do not heal an entire line alone. You do, however, change what becomes possible for the line. This is why standing in the gap often looks quiet.

It may involve refusing an old pattern. Breaking an unspoken agreement. Speaking truth where silence prevailed. Choosing obedience where compromise was customary. Ending something that everyone else tolerated. When one person stands differently, the line shifts. Maybe not immediately, maybe not dramatically, but it will change permanently.

This is also why resistance often intensifies at these moments. Bloodlines resist reordering. What has benefited from silence does not surrender easily. Resistance is not proof of the error. It is often proof of impact. Standing in the gap is not about confrontation alone; it is also about intercession.

Intercession is not pleading from below. It is appealing from position.

You appeal not because you are desperate—but because you are authorized. This is where the New Covenant matters most. You do not stand in the gap on your own merit. You stand under a greater Covenant that has already answered every lesser one.

This is not bravado; it is coverage.

Standing in the gap does not erase the past, but it does reorder the future. From there, children inherit differently, evil patterns weaken, disappointing and cataclysmic cycles lose inevitability. Permission shifts; what God allows becomes the possible in your bloodline. Amen.

This is often invisible at first. But lines remember, not everyone is called to stand in the same way. But everyone who sees clearly is called to respond responsibly. Clarity creates obligation.

This book has not been asking you to accuse your bloodline, it has been asking you to understand it. So do not fear the dark covenants in your tribe or your bloodline, but recognize which ones still speak, and which ones have already been answered.

If you are standing at a place where awareness has arrived, you are on time. You are the one called and chosen for your bloodline--, for such a time as this. For such a *tribe* as this.

Some things end with you. Some things begin with you. Some things simply change direction because you stood where you were placed. That is not pressure. That is stewardship.

A tribe is not sustained by emotion and wishes. It is sustained by people willing to stand when it would be easier to disengage. If you are reading this, you are not being asked to do everything. You are being asked to do your part. And that is enough to change a line. You are enough. Your calling is enough. Your position is enough. Your authority is enough. If you've had enough then it is time to stand in the gap, with your enough, for your bloodline. Hallelujah and Amen.

One positioned person can interrupt and cut off negative generational momentum. Standing in the gap is jurisdictional, not theatrical or heroic.

CAN YOU FIND YOURSELF IN JACOB?

This is where the book becomes spiritual, not just sociological. Jacob is not the hero of tribe-talk. He is the problem that tribe exists to solve. Jacob didn't know who he was, didn't trust inheritance. He took shortcuts to blessings. He wrestled for identity instead of receiving it. He built life through striving, not rest.

And yet—Jacob is chosen.

The question is not, *Are you Israel?* The real question is, Are you still Jacob? Can you see yourself in the name-changing, the grasping, the fear of loss, the bargaining with God, the wrestling at night when no audience is present.

Tribes are not formed at the table; they are formed after the wrestling. Jacob didn't become Israel in a group, he became Israel alone, limping, renamed, marked. Only then could a *people* come from him.

A clique wants you agreeable. A trauma bond wants you wounded. A tribe wants you transformed.

Transformation always costs ego, illusion, borrowed identity, and false belonging. This is why many people say *"tribe"*— but avoid inheritance.

This book is not asking: *Who is my tribe?*

No, it is asking: Who am I becoming fit to belong to? Am I willing to stop being Jacob— even if I don't yet know who Israel is?

POSITIVE TRAITS OF THE TRIBES OF ISRAEL

Below is a reference chart focused on the positive, adoptable characteristics traditionally associated with the Tribes of Israel (sons of Jacob). This is for Biblical pattern recognition.

The Tribes of Israel — Inherited Strengths & God-Given Characteristics

Tribe	Good Characteristics / Strengths
Reuben	Initiative, awareness, beginnings, capacity for leadership, sensitivity to consequence
Simeon	Zeal, intensity, passion when rightly governed, protective instincts
Levi	Spiritual discernment, priestly service, teaching, guardianship of holy things
Judah	Leadership, courage, praise, authority, kingship, perseverance

Tribe	Good Characteristics / Strengths
Dan	Justice, discernment, ability to judge matters, strategic insight
Naphtali	Freedom, eloquence, swiftness, joy, ability to communicate clearly
Gad	Warfare strength, resilience, courage under pressure, recovery after attack
Asher	Provision, abundance, hospitality, stability, blessing that enriches others
Issachar	Understanding of times and seasons, wisdom, counsel, discernment of strategy
Zebulun	Commerce, provision through trade, partnership, support of shared mission
Joseph (Ephraim & Manasseh)	Fruitfulness, preservation through adversity, leadership in exile, multiplication

Tribe	Good Characteristics / Strengths
Benjamin	Loyalty, courage, protection, endurance, standing firm in difficult terrain

These characteristics are not labels to claim casually, but strengths Scripture shows God developing within a people over time. Discernment—not assumption—governs inheritance.

There is good here worth inheriting. Both knowledge of that good and Wisdom are required to carry it.

COVENANT IGNORANCE IS NOT COVENANT ABSENCE

This chapter is very sobering. You don't have to *agree* with a covenant for it to affect you. You only have to be **born into its jurisdiction**.

That's why Scripture shows blessings traveling through bloodlines. It shows consequences echoing through generations. We see entire houses (bloodlines) affected by one person's vow, sin, or obedience. Some covenants are holy. Some are mixed. Some are outright **evil**.

Some were made in desperation. Some were made in famine, fear, or ignorance or under duress. So we cannot think that the quality of every covenant in our bloodline is holy, pure, or good. We cannot even think that those covenants will be to our benefit, although we wish, hope and pray that they are.

An ungodly covenant will not reflect God's heart, or the plan of God for our lives as outlined in the Bible, but they still exist **until confronted.**

Evil Covenants Are Real — and They Can Be Broken. Tribal intercessor: This is where your voice matters: Pray for your tribe.

Evil covenants can include idolatrous agreements, bloodshed-based alliances, sexual covenants, spoken vows that bound future generations, and or survival pacts made in captivity or trauma.

Scripture does not deny these. It documents them. The Bible also shows God exposing covenants. We see God overriding covenants. Our God can end covenants. This takes our participation, our repentance, prayers, decrees, declarations. It takes us walking upright in the Lord and in truth, and obedience

Take notice though: God usually starts with one person willing to ask the question. That one person is willing to stand and pray for their tribe, whoever and wherever that tribe is.

THE GENEALOGY OF JESUS

God did not bypass bloodlines to bring redemption. As said earlier, He **entered them**. The genealogy of Jesus settles this.

Jesus is traced deliberately:

- From **Abraham** (covenant promise)

- Through **David** (royal authority)

- **Into history with legal, spiritual, and prophetic legitimacy**

God explicitly says that a **man from David's bloodline will always sit on the throne.**

That means:

- Bloodlines matter

- Covenants matter

- Tribal inheritance matters

- God does not erase lineage—He **redeems it**

If bloodlines were irrelevant, genealogies would be unnecessary.

If covenants were symbolic, thrones would not require them.

- **What covenants are governing you—
  not because you chose them,
  but because you were born into them?**
- **Which ones have already been answered by Christ—
  and which ones are still operating because
  no one has named them?**

Covenants can govern you **without your consent.** They flow from your family bloodline and even from the tribe that your line hails from. From my book, **Siege:** *God Is Coming* we learn that a siege often isn't random. It's often a covenantal pressure point. A line is being contested. An is inheritance being resisted. A permission is being challenged. <u>Pray for your tribe</u>. There are covenants in place that allowed the siege. Sometimes the siege lifts not because you fought harder, but because you finally understood what you were standing in for.

Blood covenants explain why some battles repeat until someone learns to pray for their tribe.

DECLARATIVE PRAYER: I AM IN CHRIST

I am in Christ.

Not only for today.

But forever.

I am in Christ **within the line of humanity**.

I stand as one born of woman,
descended from Adam and Eve—
where life first entered the Earth,
and where death first spoke.

What was fractured at the beginning
has been answered in Christ.

Where Adam failed to guard,
Christ kept watch.
Where Eve was deceived,
Christ is Truth without mixture.

I do not deny the fall—
I stand in the redemption.

I stand in the line of Noah,
where judgment met Mercy,

where the Earth was preserved
not by human strength,
but by obedience.

What survived the flood
now answers to Christ.

I stand in the line of Abraham,
where promise was spoken before fulfillment,
where faith was credited as righteousness,
and covenant was established by God, not man.

Every promise made to Abraham
finds its yes in Christ.

I stand in the line of Isaac,
the son of promise,
where provision was revealed,
and God proved Himself as the One who provides.

I do not live by sacrifice that fails—
I live by the provision God has already made.

I stand in the line of Jacob,
the struggler who became Israel.

Where identity was contested,
Christ settles the name.

I no longer strive for inheritance—
I receive it.

I stand in the line of Judah,
where kingship was spoken,

where authority was preserved,
where the scepter did not depart.

That authority is fulfilled in Christ.

I stand in the line of David,
where covenant met throne,
where Mercy outlasted failure,
and repentance restored alignment.

The throne is answered in Christ.

I stand in the line of exile and return,
where discipline did not cancel destiny,
and restoration followed obedience.

What was scattered is regathered in Christ.

I stand in the line that leads to Jesus,
born of woman, born under law,
to redeem those under law.

He did not bypass lineage—
He entered it.

By His blood,
every lesser covenant is answered.

By His authority,
every inherited claim is judged.

By His resurrection,
every line is reoriented toward life.

I do not reject my history.
I do not fear my bloodline.
I do not deny what came before me.

I stand **in Christ** within it.

Where there were permissions not given by God,
they are revoked.

Where there were obligations fulfilled in fear,
they are released.

Where there were covenants made for survival,
they are superseded by truth.

I stand under a greater covenant.
I stand in a finished work.
I stand with authority that is not self-made.

What ends with me, ends cleanly.
What continues through me, continues rightly.
What follows me, inherits freedom.

I am in Christ—
and Christ stands in the middle of my line.

In the Name of Jesus, Amen.

DECLARATIVE LINE PRAYER — I AM IN CHRIST (WITH INHERITANCE)

I am in **Jesus Christ**—
in whom every promise is yes and amen.

I am in **Joseph**,
and I inherit righteousness, obedience, and quiet faithfulness.

I am in **Mary**,
and I inherit humility, courage to say yes to God, and the grace to carry holy things.

I am in the fathers and mothers before them,
whose names carried the promise forward.

I am in **David**,
and I inherit shepherd leadership, courage before giants, repentance that restores, and a heart after God.

I am in **Solomon**,
and I inherit Wisdom, discernment, understanding, and the ability to steward abundance rightly.

I am in **Jesse**,
and I inherit faithfulness in obscurity and the Grace to raise what I may not fully see.

I am in **Boaz**,
and I inherit integrity, redemption, kindness, and
righteous provision.

I am in **Judah**,
and I inherit praise, authority, and the preserved
scepter of kingship.

I am in **Jacob**—
Israel—
and I inherit covenant identity, perseverance, and
transformation through encounter.

There are **no enchantments against Jacob**,
and no divination against Israel.

I am in **Isaac**,
and I inherit quiet trust, provision revealed by God,
and blessing not earned by striving.

I am in **Abraham**,
and I inherit friendship with God, faith credited as
righteousness, obedience, and promise that outlives
me.

I am in **Noah**,
and I inherit obedience in a corrupt age, preservation,
and grace to carry life forward.

I am in **Enoch**,
and I inherit intimacy with God and a walk that
pleases Him.

I am in **Seth**,
and I inherit restoration of righteous lineage.

I am in **Adam**,
and I inherit God-given authority, breath, and
stewardship of the earth.

I am in **Eve**,
and I inherit life-bearing purpose and the promise
that the seed would crush the serpent.

I do not inherit fear.
I do not inherit confusion.
I do not inherit broken covenants.

I inherit what was **spoken by God**,
preserved by the New Covenant,
and fulfilled in Christ.

I am in Christ—
and in Him, my line is redeemed, ordered, and
blessed.

In the Name of Jesus, Amen.

Dear Reader

Thank you for acquiring and reading this book, I pray it has blessed you and realigned you. Of note, as soon as I finished my first read though and edit of this book, and unsolicited, my sister sent me a picture of our grandmother's (rip), great aunt who was born in 1857 and a picture of our paternal grandmother's grandmother born in 1826.

Look at God.

Most people don't need a new tribe.
They need **clarity about the one they're already in**.

I am not disconnected."

- Tribe is not found by searching outward

- Tribe is recognized by **alignment inward**

- And Christ is the only place where lineage, covenant, and belonging can settle without distortion

When you are aligned, your tribe will find you.

Shalom,

Dr. Marlene Miles

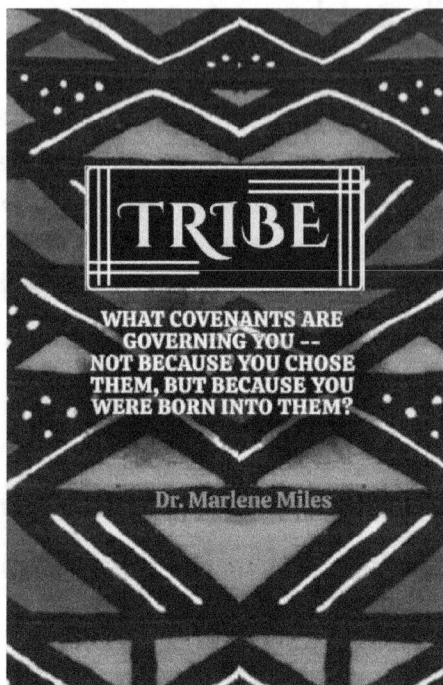

TRIBE

WHAT COVENANTS ARE
GOVERNING YOU --
NOT BECAUSE YOU CHOSE
THEM, BUT BECAUSE YOU
WERE BORN INTO THEM?

Dr. Marlene Miles

I seal these words decrees, declarations and prayers across every dimension and timeline, past, present, and future, to infinity, in the Name of Jesus.

I seal them with the Blood of Jesus and the Holy Spirit of Promise.

Any retaliation against this author, the reader or anyone who prays these prayers, makes these decrees and declarations at any time, let that retaliation backfire on the head of the perpetrator to infinity, and without Mercy, in the Name of Jesus.

Appendix: Common Tribal Distortions When Strength Is Ungoverned

Every strength becomes dangerous when it operates without restraint, accountability, or alignment with God.
Distortion is not the absence of calling—it is calling without governance.

Ungoverned Tribal Strengths — Recognizing Distortion

Tribe	Strength (Recap)	Distortion When Ungoverned
Reuben	Initiative, leadership	Impulsiveness, instability, starting without finishing, loss of authority
Simeon	Zeal, passion	Rage, cruelty, uncontrolled anger, destructiveness toward others

Tribe	Strength (Recap)	Distortion When Ungoverned
Levi	Spiritual authority, teaching	Spiritual pride, harsh judgment, gatekeeping, legalism
Judah	Leadership, praise, authority	Domination, entitlement, misuse of influence, pride in position
Dan	Justice, discernment	Deception, manipulation, hidden agendas, twisting judgment
Naphtali	Freedom, expression	Restlessness, avoidance of responsibility, lack of rootedness
Gad	Warfare, resilience	Perpetual conflict, identity built on struggle, inability to rest
Asher	Provision, abundance	Indulgence, complacency,

Tribe	Strength (Recap)	Distortion When Ungoverned
		comfort over obedience
Issachar	Wisdom, understanding	Analysis paralysis, passivity, seeing but not acting
Zebulun	Commerce, partnership	Opportunism, divided loyalty, profit over covenant
Joseph (Ephraim)	Fruitfulness, leadership	Pride in success, self-reliance, forgetting God in abundance
Joseph (Manasseh)	Preservation, legacy	Emotional detachment, burying pain instead of healing it
Benjamin	Loyalty, courage	Aggression, isolation, survivalism, loyalty without discernment

This appendix is not for accusation; it is for recognition. If a distortion resonates, do not rush to claim a tribe. Do not assume guilt. Do not self-diagnose identity. Instead, ask, What strength might this distortion be guarding? What governance has been missing? What has God been preserving beneath this pattern?

Distortion does not negate inheritance.
It signals inheritance that has operated without order. If you have found yourself or your tribe by seeing what things you've gone through or by some other recognition, then this should inform you as to how to pray.

Governance restores what chaos has obscured.

DECLARATIVE LINE PRAYER — I AM IN CHRIST

I am in **Jesus Christ**.
I am in **Joseph**.
I am in **Mary**.

I am in **Heli**.
I am in **Matthat**.
I am in **Levi**.
I am in **Melchi**.
I am in **Jannai**.
I am in **Joseph**.
I am in **Mattathias**.
I am in **Amos**.
I am in **Nahum**.
I am in **Esli**.
I am in **Naggai**.
I am in **Maath**.
I am in **Mattathias**.
I am in **Semein**.
I am in **Josech**.
I am in **Joda**.
I am in **Joanan**.
I am in **Rhesa**.
I am in **Zerubbabel**.
I am in **Shealtiel**.
I am in **Jeconiah**.

I am in **Josiah**.
I am in **Amon**.
I am in **Manasseh**.
I am in **Hezekiah**.
I am in **Ahaz**.
I am in **Jotham**.
I am in **Uzziah**.
I am in **Jehoshaphat**.
I am in **Asa**.
I am in **Abijah**.
I am in **Rehoboam**.
I am in **Solomon**.
I am in **David**.
I am in **Jesse**.
I am in **Obed**.
I am in **Boaz**.
I am in **Salmon**.
I am in **Nahshon**.
I am in **Amminadab**.
I am in **Ram**.
I am in **Hezron**.
I am in **Perez**.
I am in **Judah**.

I am in **Jacob**.
I am in **Isaac**.
I am in **Abraham**.

I am in **Terah**.
I am in **Nahor**.
I am in **Serug**.

I am in **Reu**.
I am in **Peleg**.
I am in **Eber**.
I am in **Salah**.
I am in **Arphaxad**.
I am in **Shem**.
I am in **Noah**.

I am in **Lamech**.
I am in **Methuselah**.
I am in **Enoch**.
I am in **Jared**.
I am in **Mahalalel**.
I am in **Kenan**.
I am in **Enosh**.
I am in **Seth**.
I am in **Adam**.
I am in **Eve**.

In Jesus' Name, Amen.

Prayerbooks by this author

There are some books that are only prayers. You just open up the book and pray.

Prayer Manuals

FAKE FRIENDS: *Prayers Against Betrayers*

HOLIDAY WARFARE Prayer Manual (humorous) Surviving Family Gatherings All Year Long (without catching a case)

SOUL TIE Prayer Manual (The) Part of a 3-part series including a workbook.

MAD at DADDY Prayer Manual – part of a 3-part series including a workbook.

Healing the Sibling & Relative Wound Prayer Manual

Healing the Father-Son Wound Prayer Manual

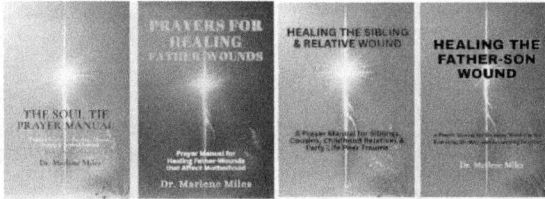

Prayers Against Barrenness: *For Success in Business and Life*

Breaking Curses of the Mother Prayer Manual

Prayers Against Barrenness: *For Success in Business and Life*

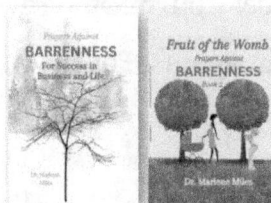

Fruit of the Womb: *Prayers Against Barrenness*

Beauty Curses, *Warfare Prayers Against*
https://a.co/d/5Xlc20M

Courts of Marriage: Prayers for Marriage in the Courts of Heaven *(prayerbook)* https://a.co/d/cNAdgAq

Courtroom Warfare @ Midnight *(prayerbook)*
https://a.co/d/5fc7Qdp

Demonic Cobwebs *(prayerbook)* https://a.co/d/fp9Oa2H

Every Evil Bird https://a.co/d/hF1kh1O

Gates of Thanksgiving

Spirits of Death, Hell & the Grave, Pass Over Me and My House

Throne of Grace: Courtroom Prayer

Warfare Prayer Against Poverty
https://a.co/d/bZ61lYu

Prayer Manuals

FAKE FRIENDS: *Prayers Against Betrayers*

HOLIDAY WARFARE Prayer Manual (humorous) Surviving Family Gatherings All Year Long (without catching a case)

Other books by this author

Abundance of Jesus (The)
https://a.co/d/5gHJVed

AK: The Adventures of the Agape Kid

Already Married in the Spirit: *Why You May Not Be Married in the Natural*

AMONG SOME THIEVES https://a.co/d/dkYT4ZV

Ancestral Powers

Anti-Karen: *How To Mind Your Own Business Without Minding Other People's*

Anti-Marriage, *The Spirit of*

Backstabbers https://a.co/d/gi8iBxf

Barrenness, *Prayers Against*
https://a.co/d/feUltIs

Battlefield of Marriage, *The*

Beware of the Dog: Prayers Against Dogs in the Dream.

Bless Your Food: *Let the Dining Table be Undefiled*
https://a.co/d/6oPMRDv

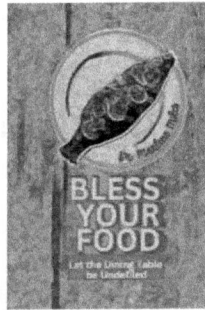

Blindsided: *Has the Old Man Bewitched You?*
https://a.co/d/5O2fLLR

Break Free from Collective Captivity

Broken Spirits & Dry Bones

By Means of a Whorish Father

Caged Life: Get Out Alive!
https://a.co/d/bwPbksX

Casting Down Imaginations

Christ of God (*The*) 3-book series

Christ of God, (*The*) Box Set, includes all three books

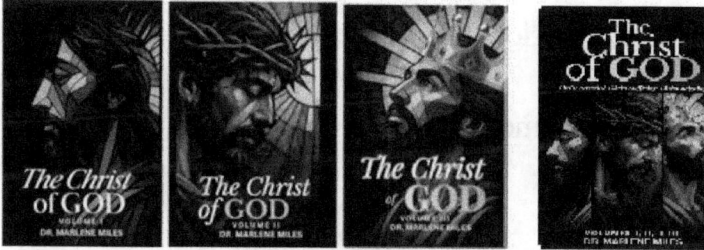

Churchzilla, The Wanna-Be, Supposed-to-be Bride of Christ https://a.co/d/eAf5j3x

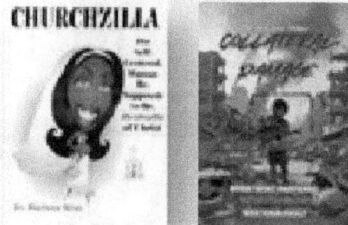

Collateral Damage: *When What Happened Spiritually Was Your Fault*

Demonic Cobwebs (prayerbook)

Demonic Time Bombs

Demons Hate Questions

Devil Loves Trauma, *The*

Devil Weapons: Unforgiveness, Bitterness,…

The Devourers: Thieves of Darkness 2

Do Not Swear by the Moon

Don't Refuse Me, Lord (4 book series)

https://a.co/d/idP34LG

Dream Defilement

The Emptiers: *Thieves of Darkness, 1*
https://a.co/d/5I4n5mc

Entanglements: Illegal Knots Limiting Your Life (new)

Evil Touch

Failed Assignment

Fantasy Spirit Spouse https://a.co/d/hW7oYbX

FAT Demons (The): *Breaking Demonic Curses*
https://a.co/d/4kP8wV1

The Fold (5-book series)

- The Fold (Book 1)
- Name Your Seed (Book 2)
- The Poor Attitudes of Money (3)
- Do Not Orphan Your Seed (4)
- For the Sake of the Gospel (5)
- My Sowing Journal

Gang Ups: Touch Not God's Anointed

Gathered: No Longer Scattered
https://a.co/d/1i5DPIX

Getting Rid of Evil Spiritual Food

https://a.co/d/i2L3WYQ

got HEALING? Verses for Life

got LOVE? Verses for Life
https://a.co/d/8seXHPd

got HOPE? Verses for Life

got money? https://a.co/d/g2av41N

Has My Soul Been Sold?
https://a.co/d/dyB8hhA

Here Come the Horns: *Skilled to Destroy*
https://a.co/d/cZiNnkP

Hidden Sins: Hidden Iniquity

https://a.co/d/4Mth0wa

How to Dental Assist

How to Dental Assist2: Be Productive, Not Wasteful

How To Stay Prayed Up

How to STOP Being a Blind Witch or Warlock

I Take It Back

In Multiplying I Will Multiply Thee

Into Freedom:

Irresistible: Jesus' Triumphal Entry
https://a.co/d/dO9IfEC

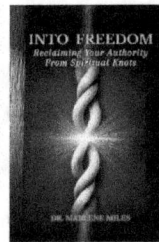

KNOW YOUR BATTLE: Stop Swinging Blindly — and Win Against Opponents, Adversaries & Enemies (Workbook) https://a.co/d/eOwFKlV

Legacy

Let Me Have A Dollar's Worth
https://a.co/d/h8F8XgE

Level the Playing Field

Living for the NOW of God
https://a.co/d/6bK5duE

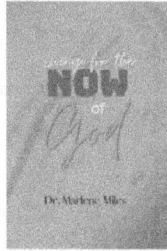

Lose My Location https://a.co/d/crD6mV9

Love Breaks Your Heart

Mad At Daddy: Healing Father-Wounds that Affect Motherhood (book, workbook & prayer manual)

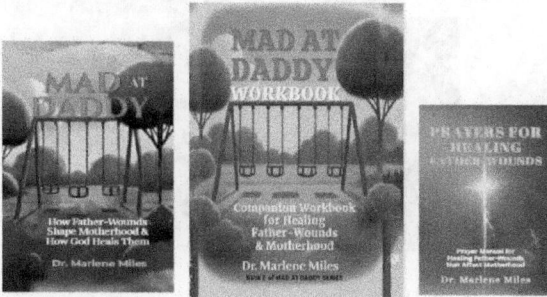

Made Perfect In Love

Mammon https://a.co/d/29yhMG7

Man Safari, *The*

Marriage Ed.: *Rules of Engagement & Marriage*

Made Perfect in Love

Money Hunters: Beware of Those

Money on the Altar https://a.co/d/4EqJ2Nr

Mulberry Tree, *The* https://a.co/d/9nR9rRb

Motherboard (The) - *Soul Prosperity Series*

Name Your Seed

Occupy: *Until I Return* https://a.co/d/bZ7ztUy

One Defining Day: *A Day When Dreams Come True*

Opponent, Adversary, or Enemy?: Fight The Right Battle with the Right Weapons

https://a.co/d/byQqEE2 & companion workbook: Know Your Battle

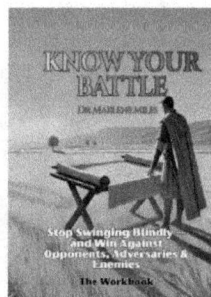

Plantation Souls

Players Gonna Play

Portals: Shut the Front Door: Prayers to Close Evil Portals.

Power Money: Nine Times the Tithe

https://a.co/d/gRt41gy

The Power to Get Wealth
https://a.co/d/e4ub4Ov

Powers Above

The Robe, Part 1, The Lessons of Joseph

The Robe, Part II, The Lessons of Joseph

Seasons of Grief

Seasons of Siege: God Is Coming

Seasons of Waiting

Seasons of War

Second Marriage, Third--, *Any Marriage*
https://a.co/d/6m6GN4N

Seducing Spirits: Idolatry & Whoredoms
https://a.co/d/4Jq4WEs

Shut the Front Door: *Prayers to Close Portals*
https://a.co/d/cH4TWJj

Siege: *God Is Coming*

Sift You Like Wheat

Six Men Short: What Has Happened to all the Men?

SLAVE

Sleep Afflictions & Really Bad Dreams
https://a.co/d/f8sDmgv

Soul Prosperity soul prosperity series 3

https://a.co/d/5p8YvCN

Soul Ties: How Soul Ties Form, and How To Break Them (book, workbook & prayer manual)

Souls In Captivity

The Spirit of Anti-Marriage

The Spirit of Poverty https://a.co/d/abV2o2e

Spiritual Thieves https://a.co/d/eqPPz33

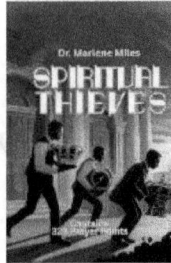

StarStruck- Triangular Power series.

SUNBLOCK- Triangular Power series.

The Swallowers: *Thieves of Darkness*, 3

Take It Back

This Is NOT That: How to Keep Demons from Coming at You

Time Is of the Essence

Too Many Wives: *Why You Have Lady Problems*

Tormenting Spirits   https://a.co/d/dAogEJf

Toxic Souls

Triangular Power *(series),* Powers Above, SUNBLOCK, Do Not Swear by the Moon, STARSTRUCK

TRIBE: *What Covenants Are Governing You...?*

Unbreak My Heart: *Don't Let Me Die*

Uncontested Doom

Ungovered Hunger: How Unchecked Appetite Dismantles Authority

Unguarded Hours, *The*

Unseen Life, *The* (forthcoming)

Upgrade: How to Get Out of Survival Mode Toxic Souls (Book 2 of series) , Legacy (Book 3 of series)

The Wasters: *Thieves of Darkness,* Bk 2
https://a.co/d/bUvI9Jo

What Have You to Declare? What Do You Have With You from Where You've Been?

When I Was A Child, *I Prayed As a Child*

When the Devourer is Rebuked
https://a.co/d/1HVv8oq

When The Table Is Set Against You

WTH? Get Me Out of This Hell
https://a.co/d/a7WBGJh

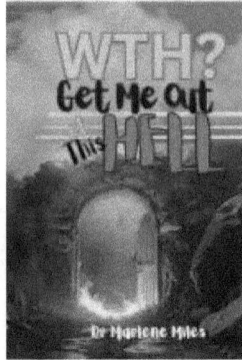

The Wilderness Romance *(series)* This series is about conducting a Godly relationship and marriage with someone who is a Wilderness person. *The Social Wilderness*

- *The Sexual Wilderness*
- *The Spiritual Wilderness*

Other Series

The Fold (a series on Godly finances)
https://a.co/d/4hz3unj

Soul Prosperity Series https://a.co/d/bz2M42q

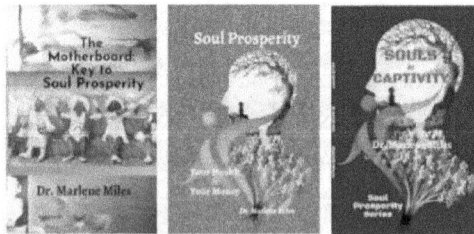

Spirit Spouse books

https://a.co/d/9VehDSo

https://a.co/d/97sKOwm

Battlefield of Marriage, The

https://a.co/d/eUDzizO

Players Gonna Play

https://a.co/d/2hzGw3N

Sent Spirit Spouse (can someone send you a spirit spouse? This book is not yet released.)

Matters of the Heart, Made Perfect in Love
https://a.co/d/7OMQW3O , Love Breaks Your Heart https://a.co/d/4KvuQLZ, Unbreak My Heart https://a.co/d/84ceZ6M Broken Spirits & Dry Bones https://a.co/d/e6iedNP

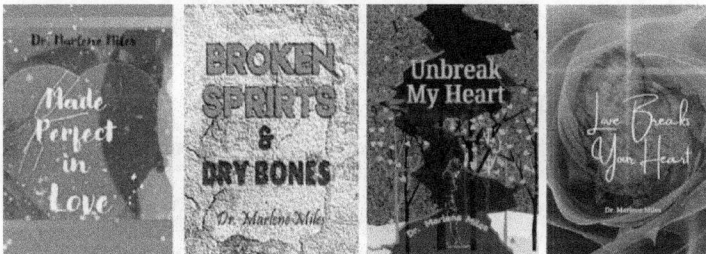

Thieves of Darkness series

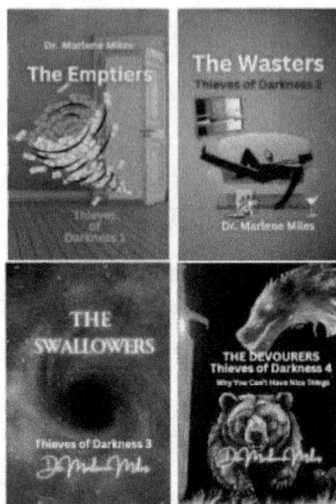

The Emptiers https://a.co/d/heio0dO

The Wasters https://a.co/d/5TG1iNQ

The Swallowers https://a.co/d/1jWhM6G

The Devourers: Why We Can't Have Nice Things
https://a.co/d/87Tejbf

Spiritual Thieves

Red Flags: The Track Is Not Safe (book & workbook)

Triangular Powers https://a.co/d/aUCjAWC

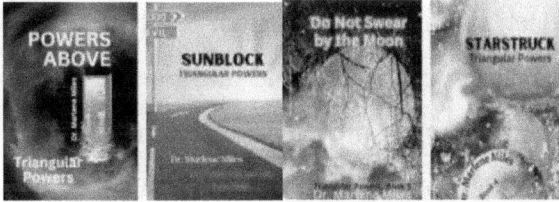

Upgrade (series) *How to Get Out of Survival Mode*
https://a.co/d/aTERhX0

We Get Along, Right? Compatibility for Couples – (book & workbook)

Dr. Marlene Miles is a teacher, author, and spiritual thinker known for her grounded, discerning approach to prayer and spiritual formation. Her work emphasizes clarity, restraint, and maturity in faith—helping believers move beyond emotionalism and performance into a steady, practiced walk with God.

With a deep respect for Scripture and a practical understanding of daily life, Dr. Miles writes for those who want their prayer life to be formed, not dramatized. Her teaching encourages spiritual maintenance, discernment, and responsibility—so faith remains strong not only in crisis, but in everyday living.